Biddy Baxter, Edward Barnes and Rosemary Gill devised and wrote The Blue Peter Book

HELLO THERE!

Here's our Eleventh BLUE PETER BOOK—our second in double figures—and this year it's been more difficult than ever choosing which of our adventures to write about.

There have been a great many celebrations. Three members of the crew of Blue Peter III, our Inshore Rescue boat stationed at North Berwick in Scotland, received top awards for bravery from the Royal National Lifeboat Institution and we won an award, too—for the fifth year running readers of the *Sun* newspaper voted us the Top Children's Programme. John flew with the RAF Flying Falcons, and with his incredible five-mile drop became Europe's Civilian Free Fall record holder.

Our Blue Peter Stampede enabled hundreds of victims of the terrible Ethiopian drought and famine to leave their refugee camp and return to their village. We were able to provide an irrigation scheme for another part of the country, too, and last April we saw the opening ceremony at Wolverhampton of our second Blue Peter Old People's Centre.

What with the squeeze and the freeze and all the economic crises, life hasn't been particularly easy during the past year. Pocket money certainly doesn't seem to be going as far as it did—that's if you're lucky enough to be given any—so we've included some ideas in this book for things to make that are really cheap! Some of them, like the fishing game and the junk jewellery, needn't cost anything

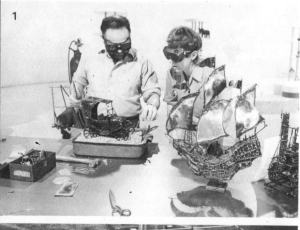

at all.

A lot of our best ideas come from *you*. On page 58 you can read about a Blue Peter viewer with one of the most unusual hobbies we've ever shown on the programme. Another viewer told us about his strange pet, and that resulted in a wild kangaroo chase with John hopping round the studio after six-month-old Macro, and Lesley trying to lure him back in front of the cameras with a newspaper full of his favourite food—fish and chips!

What with Pantomime lessons from Arthur Askey, climbing Black Crag with Chris Bonnington, and canoeing through 15-foot breakers off the Ivory Coast, it's been a pretty action-packed year. And if you'll keep on writing and giving us more of your good ideas, who knows what we'll be up to in 1975!

Valerie Singleton

John Noakes

Peter Purves   Lesley Judd

Petra   Jason   Shep

P.S. Don't forget the competition!

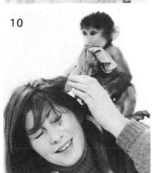

10

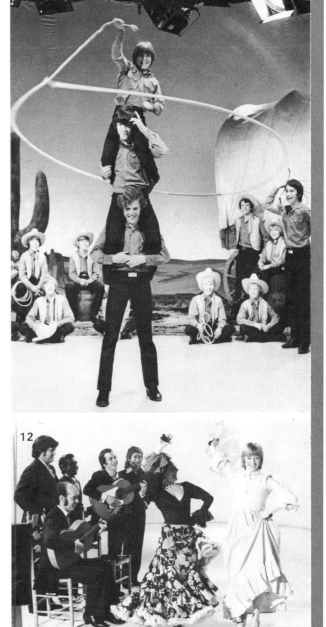

12

DEATH BEFORE·DISHONOUR

Battalion—Royal Salute—Present—Arms!
Three hundred bayonets flashed in the sun, and the band struck up the National Anthem as the Prince of Wales drove in an open Land-Rover on to the parade ground.

The occasion was the Presentation of the Colours to the Third Battalion of the Royal Regiment of Wales, but for Goat Major Peter Browning and me, it was Dewi's first big parade and we were desperately hoping that he was going to behave himself. Dewi had a mind of his own, and we were afraid he might not be so impressed by the Heir to the Throne as the rest of the Regiment.

The Land-Rover stopped and Prince Charles got out and began to inspect the lines of immaculate soldiers. As he strode across the parade ground, the Prince caught sight of Dewi. He paused for a moment and then began to walk directly across to where Goat Major Browning was standing to attention with Dewi held on the shortest possible lead. Dewi's head went down ever so slightly as his silver horn caps gleamed in the sunshine. I held my breath, but Peter didn't flinch.

Only three months before I was with Peter and Regimental Sergeant Major Pennington and Captain Martin at Whipsnade Zoo when Dewi was chosen from a herd of 15 Cashmere goats.

Nobody's quite sure when the Welsh Regiment first began to have goats for its mascots. The story goes that when the 41st Foot was starving in the Crimean war in 1855, a goat was captured and was going to be used for food, but someone called him "Billy", and after that, no one could bear the thought of killing him. "Billy" became a mascot and was the pride of the Regiment until he died in 1861. His successor was presented to the Regiment by Queen Victoria. Then in 1936 King Edward VIII gave his herd of Cashmere goats to Whipsnade Zoo, and now the Zoo supplies goats to the Regiment on behalf of the Sovereign.

The three soldiers and I waded through the herd of white, silky, bleating goats.

1 This is Dewi—mascot of the 3rd Battalion of the Royal Regiment of Wales.

2 I helped to choose him from a herd of Cashmere goats at Whipsnade Zoo.

"What about him?" asked Captain Martin. Goat Major Browning lifted up the back foot of a very handsome goat.

"Hooves are a bit soft, sir," he said.

"How about this one?" I said, picking up the prettiest kid in the whole herd.

"Very appealing, Lesley, but he's too young! In October he's got to go on Parade with the Prince of Wales, and *that* one might take a run at him."

Captain Martin pointed with his baton to a goat with a marvellous beard right in the middle of the herd. Peter singled him out and carefully examined his teeth, his coat and his hooves.

"That's the one, sir. He's perfect!"

The next time I saw Dewi was on the day before the Royal visit. "He's coming on well with his marching," Peter told me as we walked to Dewi's quarters. And in spite of exaggerated press reports asking 'Will Dewi run amuck on the big day', Peter was sure that the new mascot was going to live up to his Regimental motto—

"Death before Dishonour".

In Dewi's hut we poured half a bottle of shampoo on his back before we could get a decent lather, and it took two electric hair-driers blowing at full blast to dry him off afterwards. A whole tin of talcum powder was brushed into his coat so that Dewi was not only whiter than white, but smelled more like a ladies' boudoir than a goat enclosure.

October 27 dawned, and all three of us looked very different from the day before. Peter had abandoned his denim overalls for a glamorous red and blue uniform with a green sash across his chest. Dewi was quite magnificent in his green jacket with a silver head badge, and silver horn tips!

I changed into a long dress so as not to let them both down. We travelled by Land-Rover to Cardiff Castle where I went to find my seat among the spectators, and Peter and Dewi went to take their place at the head of the parade.

3 On the morning of the big day, I helped to give Dewi a wash and brush up.

4 It took two hair driers to dry out his beautiful Cashmere coat.

5 Goat Major Browning and Dewi went by Land-Rover to Cardiff Castle.

6 Inside the castle, Dewi waited to be dressed ready for the Parade.

7 First came the green jacket with the regimental coat of arms.

8 Then with silver horn tips, and silver head badge, Dewi was led on Parade.

9 The Prince of Wales strode across the parade ground, looked admiringly at Dewi, and talked to Peter. "What did he say?" I asked. Peter hesitated. "Well, he asked if Dewi ever made a mess on parade."

Dewi was behaving well, but I could tell he was feeling a bit nervous.

"Battalion—by the Left—Quick March!" roared Lieutenant Colonel Pim. To the tune of "Great Big David". the battalion moved off to the parade ground. Dewi, perfectly in line, high stepped in time to the music alongside the Goat Major. At last the moment we had been preparing for since early spring was upon us.

The Prince of Wales was actually there— admiring Dewi and talking to Goat Major Peter Browning.

Dewi looked at the Prince. The Prince smiled at Dewi, and Peter stood rigidly to attention.

"What did he say?" I asked, the moment the Parade was over.

"Oh, nothing much," said Peter.

"Oh, come on," I pressed. "What did he really say?"

Peter hesitated. "Well, he asked if Dewi ever made a mess on parade."

"And what did you say?" I asked.

"Well—I took a tight grip of his collar, hoped for the best and said 'No Sir'!"

Death indeed before Dishonour!

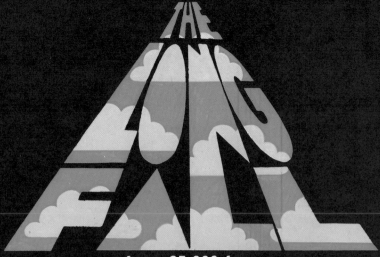

THE LONG FALL

from 25,000 feet
John Noakes tells the story from the beginning.

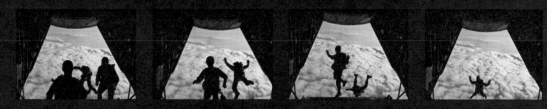

FIRST civilian in Britain to make 5 mile high free fall
FIRST television presenter in Britain to talk to camera
falling through space
FIRST "outsider" to join the Flying Falcons

To make the "high one", I had to start training from the beginning again. I hadn't put on parachuting gear for five years so I felt pretty apprehensive.

I started by leaping from a tower—

which was much more frightening than jumping out of an aeroplane!

"Were you scared?" I think that's the question that every newspaper reporter asked first.

I usually answered—"Yes, I was a bit," but I didn't tell them that I've been much more terrified with both feet on the ground in a "live" Blue Peter Studio. It seems daft, I know, but I wasn't so worried about forgetting my words at 25,000 feet!

The whole thing started seven years ago when the Flying Falcons asked me if I'd like to try a parachute jump. This was no free fall, but a straight jump with the ripcord being pulled automatically as soon as I left the aircraft. From that moment on, I knew I was hooked. I thought that floating through air on the end of a parachute was the greatest sensation on earth, but I didn't know half of it—Free Fall was still to come!

Two years later, after training with the Army Red Devils team, I leapt from the aircraft for the first time with no strings attached. For five glorious seconds I was on my own in space—"1001—1002—1003—1004—1000 and PULL!" My parachute opened and my first free fall was over. It was enough to whet my appetite for the big one.

Then no more parachuting for five long years until I had a call from Flight Lieutenant Alec Jackson, the leader of the Falcons.

"The lads and I wondered if you'd like to try the 'high one'—from 25,000 feet—unless you've given it up, that is!"

The five-mile fall is the ambition of every parachutist. Not many amateurs get the chance, because you need a lot of expensive equipment like oxygen and breathing apparatus—apart from the aeroplane to take you there!

The free fall position is first learned by hanging from the roof of a hangar like a puppet on a string.

**Into opening position—check your altimeter—
ready to pull!**

by the aircraft door, "Go" will send you hurtling
through space without a second thought or a
backward glance. But at that moment I was
swinging like a giant Andy Pandy from strings
75 feet above the asphalt parade ground.

"Legs together—elbows in—look straight
ahead!"

I remembered that from the last time. If your
feet aren't together and your elbows in, you could
easily break a bone when you hit the ground at
20 mph. I practised landings—free fall positions—
and exits from the aircraft. I learnt how to read
my altimeter and what to do when the main chute
failed. I crawled into bed every night with bruised
knees, an aching back, and "Go" echoing through
my mind.

When the day for the two-mile fall arrived, I
was so fit and I felt so much one of the team that
I almost forgot to be nervous. My main concern
was that Alec Jackson and the boys would
think I was good enough to go on for the
"high one".

The cool professionalism of the Falcons had
affected me. Every jump was a risk—only a fool
would think otherwise. But every possible safety
precaution was taken. The experience of a team
with thousands of jumps and hours of free fall was
behind me—and yet it could all go wrong. Every
member of the team accepts that, and I accepted
it too.

There was just one moment which came after
free falling successfully for 9000 feet. I checked
my altimeter, pulled my ripcord, and nothing
happened! My parachute had caught in a slight
vacuum on my back and hesitated—for the
longest two seconds of my life—before it
opened! For those two seconds, my heart boomed
in my throat with the sound of a bass drum
drowning the roaring wind as I fell towards earth
at 120 mph. These are the moments you
remember! But my parachute *did* open, and what's
more, I landed smack on target.

"Not bad, John. Let's hope you do as well from
25,000 feet!"

"You mean it's 'Go'?" I asked.

"If the wind's right and the cloud's right, and
your next course of training's right, then it could
be 'Go'," he said cautiously.

At 25,000 feet there's hardly any oxygen, and

"You'd have to train all over again, of course,"
said Alec Jackson. "Hello, are you still there?"

"Sorry, I was just putting on my parachute
boots," I said.

Training began in earnest three weeks before
the "high one" as I was now beginning to call it.
The idea was to attempt a two-mile drop with a
sixty-second delay (the time between leaving the
aircraft and pulling your ripcord) and if that were
successful, I would move on to the training for
25,000 feet with a two-minute delay.

I began with the 75-foot tower where you
swing from a platform with your parachute
harness suspended on a kind of a pulley. Strangely
enough, this was the most frightening part of the
whole thing. Seventy-five feet is just high enough
to give you the colly-wobbles—go up another
thousand feet and the ground seems so far away
as to be unreal.

"Stand against the gate—Yellow brake off!
Both hands across your reserve parachute—
And Go!!!"

"Go" is the word that rings across the
Parachute Training School from dawn to dusk.
Every move and every operation is triggered off by
that same command until at the moment of truth

**Before you jump from 25,000 feet you must learn
how to use an oxygen mask.**

At last the big day arrived and we posed for a last picture before we boarded.

No turning back now. With the rest of the team, I walked towards the aircraft.

I was No. 1. On the command "stand up", I walked to the back of the aircraft and stood by the open door.

Green light on—Go! The next second I was falling through space at 120 mph with the ground five miles below.

without oxygen you die. So the first thing to learn was how to use the breathing apparatus. Inside a decompression chamber, I found out what it was like to live for a few minutes with not enough oxygen. As the air was pumped out of the chamber, we were commanded to burp (in our own time) so as to lose some body air.

Dr Jamieson, the medical instructor, was in charge.

"Right John, just drop your mask, leaving your mike on."

At first it didn't feel any different. I'd expected to feel suffocated, but I wasn't at all.

"Now write your name and address."

Kids' stuff, I thought!

"Now will you write down the thirteen times table."

I started off all right, but gradually I got slower and slower. "Five thirteens are 65—
Six thirteens are seventy—seventy—"

I was beginning to feel muzzy.

"Six thirteens are seventy—"

My head felt heavy and my vision began to blur.

"Seven thirteens are—um—thirteen—"

"Would you put your mask on again, please," said Dr Jamieson, "and write down your name several times."

I felt really dreadful as soon as I got the oxygen back, but within a few minutes I was OK. I wrote John Noakes in enormous writing first of all and gradually as my body began to accept the oxygen again, my writing got back to normal. I was given a certificate to say I'd completed the decompression drill, and went to join the rest of the Falcons for the team briefing at Abingdon.

In the Falcons' hut Alec Jackson stood in front of a blackboard where he'd already written the stick order.

"OK. Today's the high one from 25,000 feet. Stick order as you can see is on the board. John Noakes is going out No. 1, port stick, followed by Bob with the helmet camera. Opening height, 3000 feet."

All the problems are ironed out on the ground so that once the team steps into the aircraft, every man knows exactly what's going to happen, and what he's got to do.

We moved off to the dressing-room, and as we buckled on parachutes, I began to feel the butterflies in my stomach for the first time. I checked everything about twenty times, and then my free fall instructor gave me a final ground check—just to make sure. I asked what the temperature would be at 25,000 feet.

"I should think about 30 degrees centigrade *below*."

We walked across the tarmac in a group, climbed aboard the aircraft, sat down on either side of the fuselage in correct stick order, and waited.

When I'm flying as an ordinary passenger, I always feel it takes ages to get the aircraft off the ground. But I've never known a longer journey than that short trip from RAF Abingdon to the Dropping Zone on Salisbury Plain.

At last the tailgate swung open, and there was the vast sky with Salisbury Plain just visible five miles below us.

The aircraft noise is so great, all orders are given by the Jump Master holding up a board. "Chance to walk around" it said—so we disconnected ourselves from the plane's oxygen

Linking up with Ray Willis, the free fall cameraman, I fell for 3000 feet until it was time to pull my ripcord.

supply and screwed the leads into our own bottles.

The card changed to "Stand Up". We made two neat lines facing the great open door. I put my goggles down and fixed my eyes on the lights which are controlled by the Navigator from the cockpit. I was No. 1 with eleven men behind me. There was no turning back now.

Red light on—Stand by.

Green light on—Go!

1001, 1002, 1003, 1004, 1000 and PULL!

In the free fall position—and the boys were all around me. Ray Willis, the still cameraman, grabbed my left hand, and Bob, the movie cameraman, grabbed hold of him so that he was facing me—then Henry MacDonald joined up the circle so we were all four linked together in a stable free fall position. It was very difficult to talk to the camera as my cheeks became hollow with the force of wind.

I looked up just in time to see a huge black figure hurtling towards us. As he hit my arm, I was wrenched away from Ray, and spun round and round in the air until I was upside down in space. Somehow I got back in the free fall position and looked at my altimeter—6000 feet. One by one we drifted away from each other to give ourselves plenty of air for the opening. At 3000 feet my parachute was open—this time without a hitch. As I drifted down to earth, I saw Andy Sweeney gesticulating and shouting. I couldn't hear a word—What was he on about?—something smoke? Then it dawned on me. I had a smoke canister on my leg to give the Blue Peter cameraman on the ground a chance to follow me as I came down, and I was so pleased with myself, I clean forgot to pull it. I gave it a great yank, and a trail of orange smoke jetted away from me—1200 feet to go—better late than never!

On the ground, Andy and the other Falcons clustered around me. We were all elated—high on a five-mile fall. But they are a marvellous bunch of lads. Not many world beaters would let an amateur join their ranks and accept him as one of them. They've given me the greatest experience of my life—and I'll never stop being grateful.

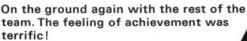

On the ground again with the rest of the team. The feeling of achievement was terrific!

BLUE PETER SPECIAL ASSIGNMENT : VENICE : SHOOTING SCHEDULE

SUNDAY MAY 6 : GONDOLA SEQUENCE WITH VALERIE & LUPETTO (GONDOLIER)

(Script pages 2 & 3)

a.m.
08.00   Motorboat arrives at the hotel's water gate to
         take Valerie and the crew plus filming equipment
         to the Riva to meet up with the gondola

08.30   Set up in gondola for interview sequence
         Valerie and Lupetto in gondola plus cameraman,
         sound recordist and director
         Remainder of unit and all unnecessary gear to follow
         at a distance in motor boat

         shooting interview sequence

         canal from Bridge of Sighs
         mente de L'Anzolo
         lo Querini Stampalia
         oon past the Doge's Palace
         etta

    nb   mente de L'Anzolo
         e gondola
         along stretch of canal
         the roof of the
    fo
    groce

12.45   All unit return to Riva   from
         gondola and break for lun

Continuity for Val : in yellow suit with b
Continuity for Lupetto: To wear gondolier's tradi

COMMENTARY:
Once there were 10,000 now there ar
100 - mostly used by tourists.
   In the fifteenth century everyone
palaces would have had its own
The families of the merchant pr
                produce richer

AME
VAL IN G

LONG

St Marks
Square

John
traine
glass
blo

Bells
St Marks

BLEEP AND BOOSTER

Ever since Bleep and Booster had joined the Space Commando Cubs, they'd seemed to be busy every second of the day. It was the badges that did it. Both boys were keen to earn as many as they could. Already they proudly displayed on their space suits the lightning flash of the Planet Pathfinders badge, the Solar Stove emblem for cooking and the two crossed Plantorisers that marked them out as gardeners. But now they were after the big stuff. Both boys had set their hearts on the coveted badges for Exploration and Initiative.

It was while they were flying with the rest of their Pack on the way to camp that a tiny dot on the scanner caught Booster's eye—a small planet that he'd never noticed before.

"Look, Bleep," he cried. "There's somewhere we've never been. Now's our chance to get two badges at once. Let's use our Initiative, dodge the others and do a bit of Exploring. We'll get both badges in one go!"

Bleep didn't hesitate. With a quick thumbs up, he swung the controls hard over and peeled away from the Commando Cubs neat flying formation.

As Bleep and Booster left their friends behind, they were unaware of the appalling dangers that lay ahead.

An hour later they touched down on a deserted flat-topped mountain surrounded by a plateau of green sand. Far away in the distance lay another cliff-like rock formation—purple this time, and covered with rough vegetation.

"There's nothing much to explore here, Bleep," said Booster, as he climbed out of the Space Pod and took a quick look round. "Let's make a camp by the purple cliff, and maybe we'll spot something interesting."

"Right," replied Bleep. "We'll leave the Pod docked here and travel light. At least, I will!" Booster's camping equipment always seemed ridiculous to Bleep. He himself carried a neat, lightweight pack containing a self-inflating space house, a solar torch, and a ray gun. On the other hand, Booster's gear weighed a ton. He insisted on carrying a brown canvas tent with poles, a large pocket knife with four blades and a spike for taking stones out of horses' hooves, and an enormous ball of string.

By the time Booster had loaded himself up, Bleep was half-way across the plateau.

"Come on Booster," he teased. "If you can get down the mountain with all that lot, you'll probably get a Strong Man's badge! Why don't you leave the string behind at least!"

Irritating though Bleep was, Booster refused to be drawn into an argument. "I don't care what he thinks," he muttered, "I like to Be Prepared!"

Two days later, at the foot of the purple cliff, the boys were packed up and ready for home. They'd had a thoroughly satisfactory exploration and had collected plenty of unusual specimens. Best of all were the curious semi-transparent globes that seemed to lie in every crevice. They could see a shadowy something inside them, but what it was they couldn't discover. Bleep had tried to open them with his ray gun, but the silvery spheres just disintegrated.

"We'll have to wait to find out what they are when we get back to Miron," said Booster. "Let's go!"

"Just a sec," cried Booster. "I think I'm getting somewhere at last." He'd been working away with the biggest blade in his knife on one sphere that seemed to have a tiny crack in it.

There was a sharp splintery sound. Then, as the globe split, Booster's cry of delight turned into one of disgust. At his feet lay a repellent snake-like creature, with a scaly collar and waving antennae.

"It's revolting! What is it Bleep? I've never seen anything so ugly!"

"I have," said Bleep grimly. "Not alive, but in a picture." He was rapidly thumbing his way through the Space Cub Manual. "Here it is! It's a Scaletron—found only on the Planet Horrendus. Booster," he gasped, his face pea green with fright, "we've landed on the worst planet in the galaxy!"

Booster grabbed the Manual and read in horror, "Scaletrons are dangerous when fully grown. Spherical eggs hatch during magnetic tidal season when all land surfaces submerge. Natural enemies Flying Leatheroids which migrate to Horrendus during the Magnetides. Season lasts from 80th Mars to 49th of Jupiter. Quick, Bleep, what's the date?"

"It's the 81st of Mars," his horrified friend gasped out. "Any second now they'll all be hatching—hundreds and hundreds of them."

"And worse than that," cried Bleep, "I can hear waves! The Magnetide's begun!"

Instinctively, Bleep and Booster turned to look towards their Space Pod and the distant mountain. It was an appalling sight. The Space Pod was there all right, but separating them from their only means of escape lay a swirling, terrifying sea. Eddies and whirlpools were whipped up by the fierce magnetic currents and floating on the spray were hundreds of Scaletron eggs.

As they bobbed near the shore, spurts of seething water crashed the spheres against the rocks where they fell in little splintered pieces. And from each cracked globe, a Scaletron monster slithered out, menacing and dangerous.

"They're only babies," gulped Booster. "I don't suppose they'll hurt us." He turned to Bleep for comfort, but to his horror he saw that Bleep's antennae were shaking with fright, as with a trembling hand he pointed out to sea.

In between the breakers they could see long snake-like necks of giant-sized Scaletrons—their scaly collars keeping their ferocious heads above the waves like built-in life-belts.

"It's the parents," cried Booster. "They've come in on the tide to collect the babies. Quick, Bleep, let's get out of here!"

"But how?" moaned Bleep. "We can't cross the water to the Space Pod, and there's nowhere to go!"

The Magnetide was already lapping round their feet. Rapidly, Booster summed up the situation.

"Grab your gear and start climbing," he ordered. "I think there's a crack in the cliff. Let's hide in there!"

Fear gave them extra strength, as they dragged themselves and their equipment up the almost sheer cliff face and squeezed through the crack.

It seemed to open into some sort of cave, pitch dark and terrifying. Bleep felt for his Solar torch but not even a flicker came as he frantically switched off and on.

"I'll try the radio," he cried, feeling in the darkness for the control knob attached to his space suit.

"Bleep, Bleep. Are you receiving me? S.O.S."

Feverishly he tried again and again to contact Miron City—but no one answered. Instinctively, both boys knew, as they tried an experimental shot with their ray guns, that they, too, would be useless.

"What's happened, Booster?" sobbed Bleep. "Why will nothing work?"

"It's the Magnetide," said Booster. "Its powerful forces are reacting against all our Miron-made equipment. Our guns and our torches and our transmitters are out of action for good. We'll never get rescued, but we mustn't give up." Bravely the boys struggled forwards through the blackness, each fearful as to where their stumbling steps would lead. Then, as they pushed on deeper into the cliff-side, they saw to their delight a tiny crack of light.

They squeezed themselves through the crack and found themselves on the cliff-top. It was desolate— just a few boulders sticking up from jet black rock. And at that moment, out of the sky something monstrous appeared. What had at first sight appeared to be just another rock on the horizon suddenly lifted into the air, and with a horrid screeching sound, and a flapping of giant wings, zoomed towards them.

"It's a Flying Leatheroid," cried Bleep. "And it's coming in to attack!"

The giant leather-winged bird swooped down with such speed that the blast from its wings knocked them off their feet. They felt its claws brush their heads as they flung themselves to the ground to hide in the scant shelter of the rocks.

"There's more of them," cried Booster. "And they all seem to be making for me. Why?"

Bleep thought rapidly. "It's your helmet,"

he gasped. "It's round and shiny. They think you're a Scaletron egg and they're trying to crack you open."

Booster was near to despair. "I can't take it off, Bleep. What can I do?"

Bleep reached into his back pack.

"I've still got something from Miron that will work," and he opened the valve on his self-inflating Space House.

In a flash, the two friends were inside, protected by its strong walls, and safely hidden from the flying monsters. The hideous noise of beating wings from overhead died down and the Flying Leatheroids gave up the hunt.

In the eerie silence, Bleep put his head carefully out of the door. "They're sitting about all over the place," he reported. "Now what do we do?"

"There's a saying on Earth," said Booster, "'If you can't beat them, join them'—and that's exactly what we're going to do. We're going to turn into a Leatheroid. Help me get my tent unpacked."

Bleep was baffled, but he knew that when his friend was in an inventing mood, it was no good asking questions.

Inside the space house, Bleep and Booster set to work. First they lashed the tent poles together with string to make a frame, then with the spike on his knife, Booster poked holes into the brown canvas. He threaded string through the holes and tied the canvas firmly to the poles.

"There!" he said, triumphantly, "that's it!"

"But what is it?" said Bleep, nervously. "All we've done that I can see is ruin your tent."

"Don't be daft," snapped Booster. "It's a pair of wings. It's about the same size as the Leatheroids and it's the same colour. It won't fool them in the light, but when dark comes, we may just get away with it."

He didn't sound too convinced himself, Bleep noticed, but in the ghastly position they were in, anything seemed worth a try.

All the time they waited for darkness, they could hear the squawks and screeches of the Leatheroids as they scrambled in the rocks cracking open Scaletron eggs. It was very unnerving, but as the light faded, the noises grew less, and finally they died away altogether.

"This is it, Bleep," Booster announced.

Stealthily, Bleep and Booster got under the home-made wing and crawled out into the dark. Keeping as close to the ground as they could, they crawled to the cliff edge. So far so good, but the real test was to come. If Booster's calculations were right, their canvas wing should just carry them across the Magnetide. If they were wrong, a hideous fate awaited them—a plunging death into the jaws of the giant Scaletrons.

Then, before the sleepy Leatheroids woke up to what was happening, Bleep and Booster stood up, ran as fast as they could and launched themselves over the edge of the cliff.

The rush of air, as they glided high above the Magnetide, knocked all the wind out of them, but the flying wing held together. Their hearts lifted as they swooped over the water, but the next second all hopes seemed dashed. With a monstrous scream, a Leatheroid, woken by the noise of their take-off, came zooming after them. It attacked from above, its huge claws ripping the canvas.

"We're losing height," yelled Bleep. "Look, the Scaletrons have seen us coming!"

Down below, two fierce heads waved on snaky necks, and every second Bleep and Booster were falling closer and closer to their open jaws. They shut their eyes and waited for the end.

There was a frightful scrunching sound—a scream and then silence. But miraculously, they were still flying! Then with a tremendous jolt, they hit something. Not water, but dry land! They'd made it, and as they struggled out of the wreck of tent poles and canvas, they saw what had happened. By a miracle both Scaletrons had snaked up out of the water and snatched the Leatheroid out of the air. The boys had escaped unnoticed as the flying monster was dragged down below the waves.

It took them some hours to reach the Space Pod, but there it was exactly as they had left it, and far enough away from the Magnetidal forces to be in perfect working order. Thankfully they flung themselves inside, ignited the engines and took off.

"I'll never sneer at your camping gear again," said Bleep. "I reckon as well as Initiative and Exploration, you've earned two more badges—Life Saver and Inventor!"

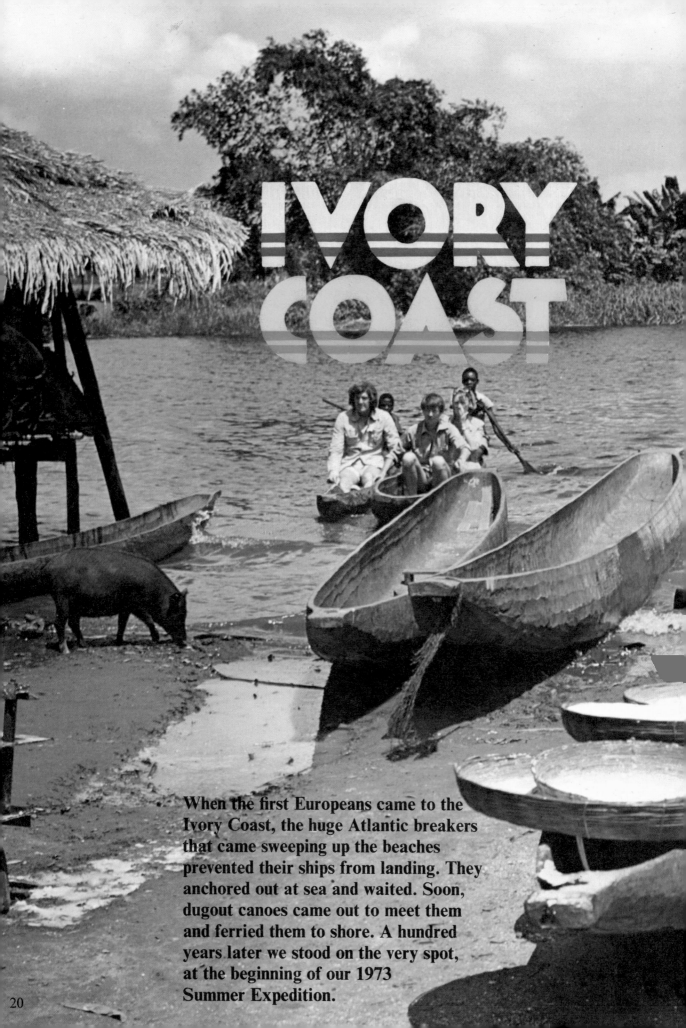

IVORY COAST

When the first Europeans came to the Ivory Coast, the huge Atlantic breakers that came sweeping up the beaches prevented their ships from landing. They anchored out at sea and waited. Soon, dugout canoes came out to meet them and ferried them to shore. A hundred years later we stood on the very spot, at the beginning of our 1973 Summer Expedition.

When we saw the size and sheer force of those breakers, we wondered how the early settlers had survived! "Still," we thought, "if they could do it, so can we," and Pete and I persuaded the fishermen of Aguerti village to take us out in their canoes to ride the surf.

That trip was unforgettable! The sea flung the heavy wooden dugout about like a cork, and as we weren't given any paddles, all we could do was hang on and hope! In seconds a solid wall of water smashed down on us, and we were flung head first into the breakers. Lesley, watching from the shore, thought we'd gone for good, but we all struggled back on board only to be capsized and nearly drowned for the second time on the way back to the beach.

Those first settlers were Frenchmen and they certainly had guts. In the early days the country was known as the White Man's Grave. Tropical diseases killed the Europeans off like flies, and we wondered what it was that brought them here and why they stayed at all. The answer was money. They came to hunt the elephant for the valuable ivory tusks that gave the country its name. Nowadays there are hardly any elephants left, and in our whole expedition we saw only one. But now there's news that the Government has banned all elephant hunting. There's a chance at last they'll breed in safety as they did in the days before the white men came.

The country is now independent, but French is still the official language. Luckily, Lesley speaks it fluently, though as soon as we went anywhere off the main road, we were in trouble. There are twenty-seven different tribal languages spoken and outside the towns hardly anyone speaks French. There's another

snag for travellers, too. Once you're off the main road, there aren't any signposts, and as you follow a track through the jungle, you've no idea if the next village is a hundred yards away or a hundred miles.

That's what made our expedition so intriguing. One day, the road just ran out by the side of a large lagoon. We hung around and then canoes came to take us to Tiegba, a marvellous village where all the houses are built on stilts. The people live by fishing, holding heavy round nets in their teeth and flinging them out to land on the water in a perfect circle. We tried, too, and discovered that if you want to come away with a full set of teeth, the moment that you open your mouth and let the net go is very critical. We didn't catch anything, but at least we kept our teeth!

At another village we came across the Yacouba tribe, where two little girls performed a death-defying ritual. Their faces were painted like masks, and when we tried to speak to them, they didn't answer. We discovered both girls were in a trance, and in a

Little dugout canoes ferried us to a village on stilts. "It's like riding in a runner bean," said Pete!

Fishing Tiegba style was tricky. John nearly lost his balance and his teeth!

strange state between waking and sleeping they danced an acrobatic ritual, balancing on the points of two razor-sharp knives. We didn't understand the

1 In Fakar village, every man's an artist, painting strange men, birds and beasts.

3 I thought this was candy floss! It turned out to be raw cotton which the ladies spin by hand.

2 The "brush" was a knife and the paint was goat dung. It stank, but it stuck well to the knife.

4 This creeper bridge swarms with stinging ants. Tradition says it must be crossed bare-foot.

was an artist. They didn't paint their pictures, though; they used knives and almost cut them into the cloth. When we tried, we found the paint had the most appalling stink. It was made of goat dung, but at least it stuck quite well to the knife, and the brown colour was very pleasing.

The funny thing is that apart from making the occasional painting into a shirt or a pair of trousers the artists never hang any of them up to decorate their houses. They use them entirely for trade, to exchange for food or tools, so to the men of Fakar village their pictures are just like money in the bank.

Something we all enjoyed specially was crossing a river on a creeper bridge. We came across it in the jungle, and we'd been told that it had to be used bare-foot. We thought we'd better follow the custom even though it was swarming with stinging ants. The bridge was made of knotted creepers. It's an extraordinary piece of engineering, as the whole thing is built in one night. No one's allowed to watch, and how the thousands of knots are made in the darkness of the jungle, goodness knows!

There was so much we discovered that was unexpected and strange to us. One thing we found out when we were home and sitting in the Blue Peter studio.

George Cansdale brought along a West African rat and we were quite pleased that we'd never actually met one face to face in the jungle! It was about the size of an average dog, and none too friendly!

"They call them 'Rabbit' in the Ivory Coast."

ritual, nor did we understand why it's the tradition for the men of the Guessesso region to dress up in elephant masks and dance on stilts. It was exciting to watch, though. The villagers ran away as the dancers approached. We thought at first that they were scared, but they weren't. They were simply sensible, because it wasn't long before one stilt man leapt just that bit too high, and came crashing down within inches of us!

It's the custom in the Ivory Coast for each village to follow one craft. We discovered one place where every man was a weaver, and another where everyone

5 This girl of the Yacouba tribe had her face painted like a mask to take part in ritual dances.

6 In a death-defying rite she was flung high in the air and balanced on sharp knives.

7 These are Balafon players—top of the pops in the remote villages.

8 This is the laundry, where we took our clothes to be scrubbed and thumped clean in a jungle river.

9 Going, going, gone! The tallest man in the Ivory Coast bites the dust!

George said casually. "I believe they make quite good eating."

We didn't say anything at the time, but we all felt a bit queasy! We'd eaten "rabbit" quite often on our Ivory Coast Expedition—and enjoyed it too! And that's something we keep finding out on our travels.

Things that seem odd and strange, or even downright nasty to us here at home, are just normal, everyday happenings to people in other countries. When you come to think of it, there's no reason why the Ivoriens shouldn't enjoy "rabbit" just as we like fish and chips!

Do you remember the day Lesley had toothache and had to stay in bed? I took over making these necklaces and bracelets, and although they look better on Lesley than they did on me, I really enjoyed making them. For one thing, they're dead easy, and for another, they needn't cost anything because you don't have to buy expensive materials. That's why I've called the necklaces and the bracelets that go with them "Junk" jewellery.

Decide how long you want your necklace to be. The "beads" are made from squares of silver kitchen foil (old foil will do if you clean it) and you'll need about 60 squares (7 cm each) for a necklace approximately 30 cm long. It's a good idea to use your first square as a pattern for all the others, but if you want smaller or larger beads, you can vary the size of your squares of foil. To make a bead, crumple a square and roll it round and round between the palms of your hands. You can flatten any sharp pieces or bumps with your fingernails. The idea is to make each ball as round and firm as possible.

Cut a length of thread about half as long again as you want your necklace to be—the extra is to allow for tying the knots. Use a needle with a large enough eye to fit fairly thick, strong thread through, and one with a fairly blunt end. Push it firmly through each bead. Thread enough beads until you've got the length you want your necklace to be—remember you've allowed extra thread at the end!

You can either leave your necklace silver or colour it by using paint. Painting's a bit messy, so make sure you put some paper on the table, and have a rag soaked in turpentine to wipe your hands on. If you remember to thread the beads loosely, you'll find you can get your paint brush in between the beads.

When you leave the beads to dry, hang them up so they don't stick to anything! You can paint the beads different colours to match your dresses. You can thread alternate large and small beads, or paint the beads with alternating colours. Small white beads next to large red ones look quite effective.

You can make matching bracelets in the same way, but thread them on thin elastic so they slip easily on to your wrist.

Lesley was delighted with her new jewellery— it even made her forget her toothache! And this junk jewellery would be ideal for the summer— it's so light it weighs almost nothing in a suitcase and you could even wear it when you went swimming and it wouldn't spoil.

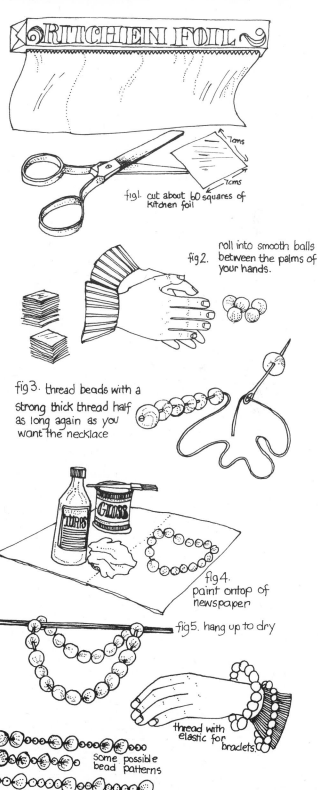

fig 1. cut about 60 squares of kitchen foil

fig 2. roll into smooth balls between the palms of your hands.

fig 3. thread beads with a strong thick thread half as long again as you want the necklace

fig 4. paint ontop of newspaper

fig 5. hang up to dry

thread with elastic for bracelets

some possible bead patterns

MACRO THE MIGHTY

Macro is the unusual and highly unpredictable pet of Zoo Curator Peter Dickenson.

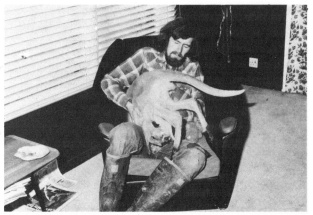

At six months, he's fairly manageable—but Macro will soon be too big for games like this.

If you were given the job of looking after a six-month-old baby who could jump one metre in the air, I wonder how you'd get on?

We didn't do too badly when Macro—the fish and chip-eating baby kangaroo—visited the *Blue Peter* studio, but we had an awful lot of exercise chasing him round our shelves when he started to get restless. Macro didn't seem to understand "sit" and "stay" like Petra and Shep, but joking apart, to come across a totally tame kangaroo baby was quite remarkable and something that would be highly unlikely to happen in the wild.

The reason for Macro's tameness was that his mother had died when he was only nine weeks old. Ever since then, he'd been hand-reared, and

consequently had absolutely no fear whatsoever of human beings.

The man who took over the job of being Macro's mother is Peter Dickenson of Lincolnshire's Cleethorpes Zoo. It's thanks to Mr Dickenson's devoted care that Macro survived, and it involved actually taking the baby kangaroo into his own home to live with him.

Macro's bed is in Mr Dickenson's kitchen and he soon became thoroughly at home. When he was tiny, he slept inside a canvas holdall bag— it probably reminded him of his mother's pouch. When he grew too big for this, he slept *on* the holdall, and for meals he liked to sit at the kitchen table. In the wild, baby kangaroos feed from their mothers until they're about one year old, and occasionally have a nibble at some grass. When he first started rearing him, Mr Dickenson fed

Most animals don't find it easy to move fast on our slippery studio floor, but Macro managed to clock up tremendous speeds.

At home Macro sits up to table for his meals. His favourite dish is fish and chips, closely followed by apple crumble.

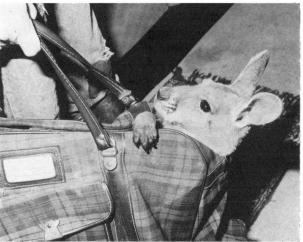

When he was tiny, Macro slept in this canvas hold-all—a sort of kangaroo's carry-cot. Now he's bigger he sleeps on it.

Macro on milk and cereal, giving him eight feeds each day. He soon found kangaroos have huge appetites, and Macro took a liking to Mrs Dickenson's cooking—especially tea and coffee and apple crumble. But his number one favourite is fish and chips—something he certainly wouldn't have tasted in the wild in Australia.

As well as having the complete freedom of the Dickensons' house, he was allowed to explore the garden, too. He's exceedingly curious and pokes his nose into everything he finds strange or unusual. But he's not at all aggressive, and has made great friends with the geese and ducks.

Eventually though, Macro will be too big and strong to continue to live as one of the family. Although he was only as long as a little finger when he was born, he'll probably end up two metres tall, and weighing about 150 lbs.

One swipe of his front legs could injure or even kill a full-grown man, and his powerful back legs will provide enough spring to send him leaping over the ground at a speed of over 30 miles per hour. At six months, Mr Dickenson said Macro had already clocked up speeds of 20 miles per hour—so it was no wonder he was so hard to catch when he started hopping round our *Blue Peter* studio.

But lured by a tasty chip, Macro came back to his seat in front of the cameras, and we thought that, considering his age, he'd been very well behaved!

It was an extraordinary experience being so close to a real live kangaroo. And with kangaroos becoming less common in certain parts of Australia, where they're treated as vermin and shot on sight, it's good to know that Macro will grow up safely, and help to preserve the species.

A SPOONFUL OF PADDINGTON

by Michael Bond, Illustrated by "Hargreaves"

Running his paw down a column on the left-hand edge, he stopped at a vacant spot, exchanged the object for a felt pen, and carefully wrote in the words: EGGSPERRYMENT NUMBER FOURTY-SEVEN— MARMALADE AND BAYKING POWDER MICKSTURE.

After a moment's thought he gloomily added the word FAYLED, and was about to underline it several more times for good measure, when he happened to glance up. The whole operation had taken rather longer than he'd expected, and catching sight of the time he dropped the pen and hastily donned his duffle-coat and hat. Shortly afterwards, having been into the kitchen in order to say goodbye to the rest of the family, he disappeared out through the front door as fast as his legs would carry him.

Paddington wasn't the sort of bear to remain down in the dumps for long, even when things weren't going his way, but all the same he wore a very disappointed look on his face indeed as he hurried down the road in the direction of the market.

But Paddington wasn't the only member of the Brown household to be unhappy about the result of the afternoon's work. The front door had hardly closed behind him when Mr Brown put down a tea towel he'd been using and held up a badly bent spoon for everyone to see.

"What on earth's happened to this?" he exclaimed. "Just look at the state it's in. Anyone would think it had been put through the mangle backwards."

"Oh, dear!" Mrs Brown looked up anxiously from her sink. "That's the third one today." She felt in the soapy water. "And here's another one. It's a good thing they're not part of our best set."

"If you ask me," said Mrs Bird, their housekeeper, "it's got something to do with that television programme we saw. The one everybody's talking about. That one with Uri Geller. I've heard lots of strange tales ever since. People's watches stopping for no reason at all, and goodness knows what else."

Jonathan and Judy exchanged glances. "I think," said Judy, "it's probably got rather more to do with Paddington."

"He's got a touch of the Uri Geller's himself," agreed Jonathan.

"He didn't have much luck reading our secret messages," continued Judy, "so he's been trying spoon-bending instead. Only it's a bit difficult with paws. He keeps on bending the handles by mistake . . ." Her voice trailed away as she caught sight of the look on her father's face.

"You must admit, Henry," said Mrs Brown, pouring oil on troubled waters, "that you were quite keen on it yourself at the time. I saw you having a quiet go with the coffee-spoons afterwards."

Mr Brown fell silent. He had to agree that like

Dipping his paw into a bowl of rather gritty orange-coloured liquid standing on a table beside his bed, Paddington shook off some loose drips which had stuck to his fur, and picked up a small silvery object lying near by.

Giving it a hard stare, he rubbed it vigorously for several minutes and then, as his whiskers started to sag under the strain, he held it up to the light and surveyed the result of his labours before turning his attention to a large sheet of squared paper spread out across the bed.

most people he'd fallen under the spell of Uri Geller, and that like most people he'd also joined in the general argument afterwards as to whether his many feats, performed under the close scrutiny of the television cameras and millions of viewers, were the result of simple, but brilliantly performed magic, or some kind of supernatural powers beyond anyone's understanding.

"Being keen is one thing," he said at last. "Bending all the cutlery is another. We shan't have any left at this rate." He held the spoon under the hot tap. "What on earth's he been putting on them . . .glue?"

"I expect it's one of his special mixtures," said Jonathan. "I think he read that someone had a theory about chemicals being used."

"*Chemicals*!" Mrs Bird gave a snort. "There are more things in heaven and earth than we've ever dreamed of," she added darkly. "Some people won't even believe the evidence of their own eyes."

"I don't know about Paddington having a touch of the Uri Geller's," said Mr Brown, wiping his hands on a towel. "It feels more like the Uri Gaga's to me." He gave the offending item a closer inspection. "Marmalade!" he exclaimed in disgust. "Dried marmalade! No wonder that bear was in a hurry to leave."

If Mr Brown had been able to share some of Uri Geller's special powers at that moment Paddington might well have reappeared at number thirty-two Windsor Gardens rather quicker than he'd left. But in saying he'd gone out in a hurry solely because of the state of the cutlery, Mr Brown was, for once, doing him an injustice.

As it happened, Paddington had several very good reasons for being in a hurry.

To start with, there was less than an hour to go before *Blue Peter* was on the air. Paddington rarely missed a *Blue Peter* programme, and the one that day promised to be even more interesting than usual, for it had been announced that as a follow-up to Uri Geller's recent appearance, viewers with similar experiences in other parts of the country had been invited to the studios to take part.

But the main reason for Paddington's haste was the fact that earlier in the day he'd received an unexpected, but obviously urgent invitation to join his friend, Mr Gruber, for tea.

Mr Gruber kept an antique shop in the Portobello Road. Paddington often called in for his elevenses in the mornings, but apart from occasional outings, it was very rare for them to have tea together, and he was looking forward to it.

Mr Gruber already had the crockery laid out on a small table at the back of his shop when Paddington arrived. He seemed to have something on his mind, but it wasn't until they had settled themselves on the horse-hair sofa reserved for such occasions that he actually got down to the subject in hand.

Clearing his throat, he glanced at Paddington over the top of his glasses. "Er, Mr Brown," he said. "I've been wondering if you would be kind enough to do me a favour?

"A young niece of mine arrived unexpectedly today, and I've promised to take her round London this evening and show her some of the sights. The trouble is," and here Mr Gruber began to look even more embarrassed, "she's brought my little grand-nephew, Ambrose, with her. We can't very well take him with us, and we've no one to leave him with . . . so I was wondering if you could possibly baby-sit for us?"

Paddington nearly dropped his cup of tea with surprise. Over the years Mr Gruber had done many things for him, and he was only too pleased to have the chance of doing something in return.

"It's very kind of you," said Mr Gruber. "I shall rest easy in my mind now. We shall be going along Windsor Gardens—I want to show my niece where you live, so I can call in and tell Mr and Mrs Brown where you are. But I thought I would ask you first. I wouldn't want you to think I was going over your head."

Having settled the matter, Mr Gruber cleared away the tea things and led the way upstairs.

Mr Gruber's niece looked at Paddington rather doubtfully as they were introduced. There was still some marmalade mixture left on his whiskers, and she couldn't help but notice that his paw was definitely sticky to the touch.

"Have you had much experience?" she inquired dubiously.

"Well," said Paddington, raising his hat politely with his other paw. "Yes, and no."

"Mr Brown is a very experienced bear," said Mr Gruber hurriedly. "And *very* reliable."

Mr Gruber went on to relate some of Paddington's past adventures, and his niece began to look slightly more impressed. She hadn't met many bears before and one couldn't always go by appearances.

"Well, I hope Ambrose is good," she said. "He's

just reached the stage when he's into everything, so I'll leave him in his pram just to be on the safe side."

Mr Gruber picked up a cardboard box. "I've collected some odds and ends from the shop," he announced, emptying the contents onto the flat canopy of the pram. "They should keep him amused."

"I've put some food out," broke in his niece. "It's all ready, so there's no need to do any cooking."

"And if you do get stuck," added Mr Gruber, as they made ready to leave, "you'll find a book of instructions on the table."

Paddington felt most important as he leaned out of the upstairs window and waved goodbye to the others. He'd never actually been left in charge of anyone before, and what with that and the thought of the *Blue Peter* programme to come, he was very much looking forward to his evening.

But his pleasure was short-lived, for just as he was giving a final wave something sharp and heavy hit him on the back of his head. He looked round just in time to see one of Mr Gruber's odds and ends, in the shape of a toy building brick, roll under the table.

Paddington gave the occupant of the pram one of his hardest ever stares. Almost immediately he had

cause to regret his action, for an ear-splitting howl rent the air. It sounded like a mixture of a faulty ambulance siren and someone undergoing some kind of severe and unmentionable torture. But what was even worse was the fact that it showed no sign whatsoever of stopping.

It was so loud and piercing it caused a number of passers-by in the street outside to stop and look up in alarm.

Closing the window, Paddington hopefully consulted Mr Gruber's instruction book. But as he turned the pages his face began to fall. It was a large and rather rambling book, and it had obviously been written in a more leisurely age for those who not only had a lot of time on their hands, but who also owned a very different baby from Ambrose. In fact, the one they had used in the illustrations looked as unlike Ambrose as chalk from cheese. Whereas the one in the book seemed to spend most of its life lying on its back with its legs in the air, gurgling happily as the author whispered sweet nothings into its ear, Ambrose was sitting bolt upright, and was clearly all set to yell his head off for the rest of the evening. Not even the sweetest of nothings seemed likely to divert him from his aim, and the only good thing about the situation was the knowledge that he was firmly strapped into the pram, otherwise there was no knowing what might have happened.

Paddington glanced anxiously at Mr Gruber's clock. Come what may, he was determined to watch the *Blue Peter* programme, but with the hands coming up to ten minutes to five matters were beginning to get a trifle desperate.

Paddington was a great believer in food during times of trouble, and having switched the television set on to warm up, he emptied the contents of a tin of strained apple into a bowl, mixed in an extra-large dollop of marmalade for good measure, and grabbed a spoon from a small pile on the canopy of the pram.

He was only just in time, for no sooner had he placed the bowl on Ambrose's lap than the familiar strains of the *Blue Peter* signature tune started up and the opening picture appeared on the screen.

To his relief the diversion seemed to have an almost magical effect on Ambrose, for he fell silent almost at once. Feeling rather more pleased with himself,

beaming at him through a thick layer of strained apple and marmalade; it was the object he was clutching in his hand.

Imitating the people on the television screen, he was rubbing his spoon with his other hand, and even as Paddington watched it began to bend in the middle until the business end was almost at right angles to the handle itself.

But there was an even bigger surprise to come. Torn between watching *Blue Peter* and keeping an eye on Ambrose, Paddington stole a quick look at the screen again. When he turned back, Ambrose had discarded the first spoon and was now hard at work doing exactly the same thing to a second one.

Paddington rubbed his eyes in order to make sure he wasn't dreaming, and in the short time they were closed yet another bent spoon added itself to the pile in the pram. From the gurgles of delight which rose from Ambrose it was clear that the baby who'd played such a leading part in Mr Gruber's book would need to look to its laurels if it ever came up against him in a 'Happiest Child of the Year' contest.

Paddington came to a decision. Mr Gruber's shop was within walking distance of the BBC Television Studios, and with nearly twenty minutes of the programme still left he was certain he could make it in time.

The *Blue Peter* team had said they were anxious to hear from viewers with unusual experiences of spoon-bending, and Paddington felt sure they would be more than interested in Ambrose's efforts. Not even Mr Geller at his peak had ever managed to bend his spoons at quite such a rate.

If the inhabitants of West London felt any surprise at seeing a pram hurtle past, propelled by a small figure in a blue duffle-coat, they showed no sign. Or if they did, Paddington was going much too fast to notice.

Paddington grabbed a nearby stool and settled down to watch the programme.

It began with a preview of the spoon-bending item to come. John, Peter and Lesley were shown seated amongst a group of other participants. They were all busily rubbing away at various shapes and sizes of spoons, and if the sighs and grunts were anything to go by, they were no nearer success than Paddington had been earlier in the day. In fact, he was just beginning to wish he'd brought some of his own spoons along so that he could join in too, when he heard a commotion going on behind him.

"'poon!" cried Ambrose. "'poon! 'poon!"

Paddington glanced round and then nearly fell backwards off his stool with surprise. The cause of his astonishment wasn't the sight of Ambrose

He hardly stopped running until he reached the Television Centre, where he found his progress barred by a burly commissionaire.

"You can't bring that pram in here," said the man sternly. "For all I know you might have a bomb hidden inside."

"'poon! 'poon!" cried Ambrose. And waving his latest effort in the air, he gave vent to his most piercing yell to date.

The commissionaire shifted uneasily as Paddington launched into a hurried explanation of why he was there. It all sounded highly unlikely, but as he peered inside the pram and saw all the bent spoons his expression changed.

"Sounds more like a bomb*shell* to me," said a second commissionaire. He held up his hands to his ears as Ambrose's yells grew even louder at the sight of all the faces. "I should let them in if I were you."

There was a flurry of movement from the cameras

and microphone booms as Paddington and Ambrose were ushered into the *Blue Peter* studio. The programme was drawing to a close, but even so the technicians rapidly took up fresh positions so that they could cover the situation.

It was a movement which was more than echoed at number thirty-two Windsor Gardens as everyone crowded round the television receiver.

"Ambrose!" cried Mr Gruber's niece.

"Paddington!" gasped the others.

"What on earth's he up to now?" exclaimed Mr Brown.

"Oh, gosh!" groaned Judy, as a close-up shot of a spoon appeared on the screen. "Don't say he's at it again!"

It was hard to tell who was the most surprised— Mr Gruber and his niece, who hadn't long left Paddington and Ambrose; or the Browns, who had only just been told what Paddington was supposed to be doing. They all watched in silent fascination as the

camera zoomed out slowly to reveal Ambrose hard at work on his spoon-bending act. He seemed to be enjoying the fact that he was the centre of so much attention, and a moment later John, Peter and Lesley came into view as they crowded round to offer their congratulations.

"I've heard of people getting the bends," said John admiringly, "but this is ridiculous."

"It's phenomenal," agreed Peter and Lesley.

"It's stewed apple and marmalade," said Paddington.

"It's a fake!" exclaimed Mr Gruber.

To everyone's astonishment he jumped to his feet and rushed towards the door. "I think perhaps I'd better make a quick telephone call," he announced. "I'm afraid young Mr Brown's a victim of one of my joke spoons!"

* * * * * * *

Mr Gruber stood in the middle of the deserted *Blue Peter* studio and held up a spoon. He rubbed it gently near the middle, and there was a round of applause as it slowly bent in two.

"I'm afraid it's part of a job lot I bought the other day," he said rather sheepishly. "It isn't one of my normal lines, but after that television programme the other evening I got the feeling that quite a lot of people might be wanting to fool their friends and pretend they could do the same thing as Uri Geller. But unlike Mr Geller's spoons this one has a hinge in the middle."

"I told you there are more things in heaven and earth than we've ever dreamed of," said Mrs Bird.

"I don't think I've ever dreamed of a spoon with hinges," said Paddington in amazement.

"You nearly fooled eight million viewers," said Lesley.

"Not to mention all of us," chuckled John. "It's a good job your telephone call came through when it did. Otherwise our switchboard would have been swamped."

Mr Gruber nodded. "On the other hand," he said, "you can fool all the people some of the time, and some of the people all the time . . ."

"But you can't fool all the people all the time," agreed Peter. "The truth will always come out in the end."

John gazed at the spoon in Ambrose's hand, and then at the remains of his apple and marmalade. "All of which," he said, rubbing his stomach, "makes me feel hungry. I vote that after we've shown Mr Gruber's niece round the studios we all go out for a meal in a Chinese restaurant."

"A *Chinese restaurant*?" Among the cries of surprise which greeted this remark, Paddington's voice was by far the loudest. All the same, he licked his lips in anticipation, for it sounded a very good way indeed of rounding things off.

"Chinese restaurants," said John with a straight face, "have chop-sticks. I don't suppose even Uri Geller himself could do anything with those."

"Glug!" gurgled Ambrose happily as he handed Paddington the last of the spoons. "Glug! Glug! . . . 'poon! 'poon! Glug!"

"And you can't," said John, amid general agreement, "say fairer than that!"

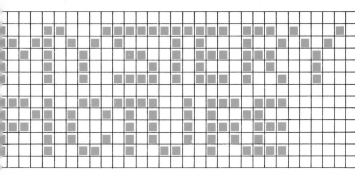

Colour the spaces as indicated by the numbers and the mystery picture will appear.

1 Light Blue   5 Light Green
2 Dark Blue   6 Dark Green
3 Red   7 Black
4 Yellow   8 Pink

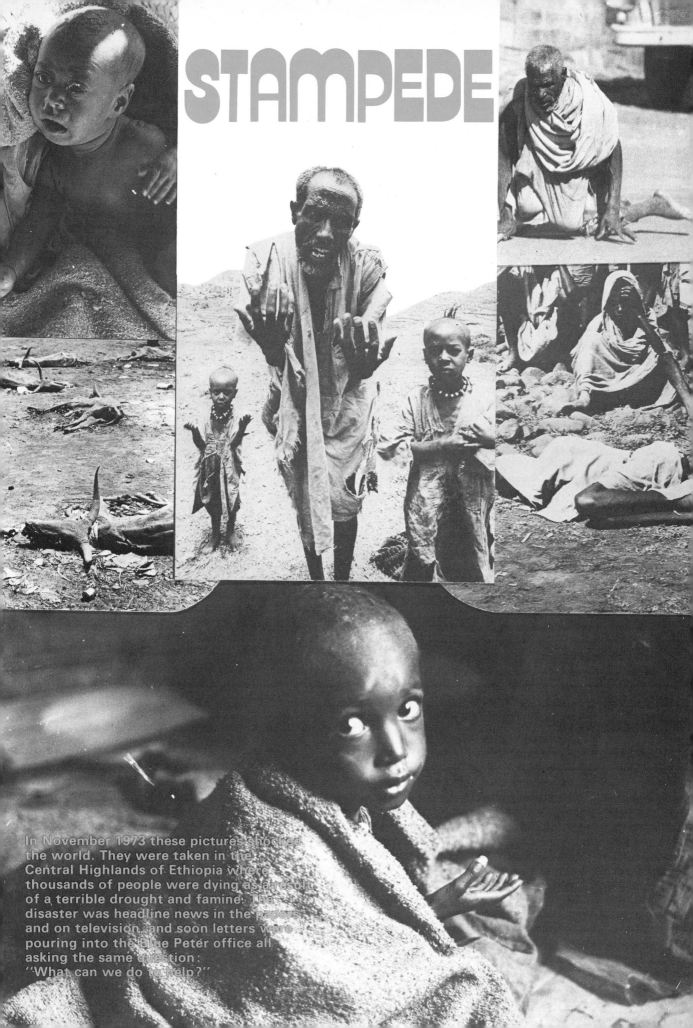

STAMPEDE

In November 1973 these pictures shocked the world. They were taken in the Central Highlands of Ethiopia where thousands of people were dying as a result of a terrible drought and famine. The disaster was headline news in the papers and on television, and soon letters were pouring into the Blue Peter office all asking the same question: "What can we do to help?"

BLUE PETER STAMPEDE

At our Stampede Depot, sorters divided millions of stamps into different categories.

The answer was our Blue Peter Stampede. We discovered that by collecting used postage stamps, badly needed aid could be given to refugees from one of the 17 camps set up to shelter the starving people. The camp was at Kombolcha and in it there were many families who had fled from their village of Dinser. The people had *had* to leave their homes because their oxen had died in the drought, and they could no longer plough their land. Their only means of supporting themselves had vanished and they were literally starving to death.

Some of the 400 Blue Peter oxen. Each ox had to pass a thorough medical examination before it was selected.

As the news reached the outside world, aid was sent to the camps. Volunteer teams of nurses and doctors launched a massive programme of curing the sick, and the people who had not died began to recover. But with the end of one problem came the beginning of another. The refugees who had survived, longed to return to their homes, but how could they, when all their possessions had been sold?

We asked the advice of the doctors and nurses at Kombolcha, and they all agreed that the best way Blue Peter could help would be to sell our stamps to buy oxen, ploughs and seed. 300 oxen, 150 ploughs and 12 tons of seed would mean that hundreds of families could return to their homes and begin new lives. And we worked out that if Blue Peter viewers sent us two million envelopes containing between 100–150 stamps,

we'd be able to achieve our target.

The scenes at our Stampede Depot were fantastic. Mail bags full of envelopes and parcels arrived at the rate of 395 per day. By the end of December we'd reached our two million target—and by mid-January we found we'd exceeded it by so much, we could not only provide an extra hundred oxen and fifty ploughs, but also a completely new project—an irrigation scheme for another part of the drought stricken area. Experts told us that the main problem was not lack of rain, but the lack of a means to conserve the water. During the "big" August rains, torrents of water pour from the skies carrying all the precious top soil before it. With no dams or irrigation channels, as fast as the rain falls, it disappears. We were told that a scheme of dams and irrigation channels in another part of the country, the Danakil Desert, could bring help to the Afars, tribes of nomadic herdsmen.

But collecting the stamps was only half the battle. Next came a desperate fight against time to make sure the oxen reached Dinser by mid-March—so that the land could be ploughed in time for the sowing season.

This couldn't be done by remote control. It needed expert planning, and we were lucky because Tony Hall, our on-the-spot reporter at

This is how we journeyed to Dinser. We were part of a 24-mule train and as well as us, there was the camera crew, Tony, Bill & Kath Taylor—two missionaries who were also trained nurses—interpreters to translate, and guides. There was a whole load of equipment and camping gear to be packed on to our mules. This was a skilled job. Mules look deceptively fragile, but they are capable of carrying huge loads, provided the weights are evenly distributed.

When we arrived at Kombolcha Camp the children ran out to meet us and Tony Hall, our on-the-spot reporter introduced us to some of the families who would be returning to Dinser with their Blue Peter oxen and ploughs.

As we set off, neither Lesley nor I knew exactly what to expect. The countryside and scenery were unlike anything we'd ever seen on any of our Blue Peter Expeditions. We crossed mountains 5000 feet above sea level, descended into dry river beds, covered mile after mile of wild scrubland, and throughout our day-long ride, there was a new breathtaking view at every glance.

Kombolcha, agreed to help. The oxen selected by Tony were gathered together in a special compound at Kombolcha. Here they were thoroughly checked and examined and given injections against diseases like rindapest.

When Dr Makonnen, the vet, finally finished his examinations, Tony supervised what was well and truly a *real* Stampede. Our Blue Peter oxen had to make the journey from Kombolcha to Dinser on hoof. It involved a day-long trek over countryside where there were no roads or even cart tracks. Just rough foot paths or dry river beds to walk along. Dinser is so isolated that before the famine, most Ethiopians did not know of its existence. Living in an overcrowded country like Britain, it's hard to imagine such isolation. Although Dinser is described as a "village", it can't be compared with anything over here. It

covers an area about 10 miles in diameter, and consists of about 18 separate collections of homes. Each group has a different name, but together they form Dinser.

Tony supervised the distribution of the oxen very carefully. The chiefs or "chickashooms" and elders of each group of huts, put forward lists of names of the people chosen to receive help. Before the big day arrived, Tony talked to all the leaders, explaining that we wanted to help only those who had no oxen and had lost all their possessions in the drought. He said he relied on the chiefs to make sure that the better off did not rob the poor, and at a swearing-in ceremony, the chiefs had to swear on the Koran in front of witnesses that the names they had given were all heads of families who had no oxen.

At the handing-over ceremony, three certificates were prepared for each oxen saying that at no time could payment be asked for them. They were

At Dinser, Tony introduced us to Said Imam and his wife and family. The last time Lesley and I had seen Said was on a film report of Tony's four months earlier in Kombolcha camp. "What do you want?" Tony had asked. "To return to our home," said Said Imam. "If only I had oxen and a plough we could all return." It was a marvellous sight to see the family rehabilitated. It didn't matter that Lesley and I couldn't speak Amharic, and that Said Imam knew no English. His face told us all we needed to know—he looked the happiest man we'd ever seen.

a gift—provided they were well looked after.

One by one, the names were called out. Each villager promised in front of the chief that he would look after his ox and not kill or sell it, and each one sealed the bargain with a thumb print on the certificate.

To the refugees and to everyone at the ceremony, the distribution of the oxen was an almost unbelievable sight. One chief said: "You know, this is a dream come true. We never thought you would really do it!"

But Tony said his best moment of all was when one man cried with delight as his huge long-horned ox came lumbering towards him. "I dreamed of such an ox last night!" he shouted and he gave his ox a name there and then, and set off joyfully for his hut.

Last March, we flew to Ethiopia with Blue Peter cameras so that people all over Britain could see for themselves exactly what their stamps had achieved.

There was no doubt that our Stampede had been an overwhelming success. And although it would be quite wrong to think that the whole dreadful problem of the drought has been solved, in one corner of the country at least the people have been rehabilitated, reunited with their friends and relations, and given a will and a way to pick up the threads of their old lives.

We hope our irrigation scheme planned for another part of the distressed area will be as successful. And it's amazing to think that used old stamps should have such life-giving power!

This was the great moment we'd been waiting for—Blue Peter oxen in action! Said Imam allowed me to lend a hand with his ploughing, ready for the sowing of the sorghum and teff seed a few weeks later.

B-504 BLUE PETER 2 R.N.L.I.

THE LIFE SAVERS

The Royal National Life-boat Institution is the world's oldest national Life-boat service. Since it was founded in 1824, it has saved nearly 100,000 lives, and in 1974 its fleet of 134 Offshore Life-boats, 111 Inshore Life-boats and 29 Life-boats in the relief fleet patrols 7000 miles of British Isles coastline.

Four of these boats have been provided by Blue Peter viewers, and this year, during the Royal National Life-boat Institution's celebrations for its 150th Anniversary, our *Blue Peter II* was put on display at a special Life-boat exhibition at London's Science Museum.

Ever since we bought our four Blue Peter Inshore Life-boats, we've been interested in the fascinating story of how life-boats were invented, and how the life-boat service started, and we discovered the first boat designed to do rescue work was built at Bamburgh in Northumberland as long ago as 1786. Joseph Lukin converted a simple fishing coble—like the one Val used when she visited the scene of Grace Darling's famous rescue—and lined it with cork to make it more buoyant. But today's life-boats are much bigger and stronger than Lukin's coble—they have to be to withstand the roughest of winter seas. They're descended from a boat that was built in South Shields, and whose design was so successful that within a few years there were

life-boats operating all round the coasts of Britain.

The South Shields boat was the result of a competition. A terrible shipwreck had taken place in 1789 when a coalship called "The Adventure" was driven aground at the entrance to the Tyne and was battered to pieces by the huge waves. People on shore watched in horror as the wretched sailors climbed the rigging and cried for help. But no boat could venture out and survive the stormy seas. One by one the sailors were dashed into the water and drowned.

Some of the onlookers were members of a Social Club called the Gentlemen of the Lawe House, and they decided to hold a competition for the best design for a life-boat to prevent such a tragedy ever happening again. One of the people who entered was William Wouldhave, a 38-year-old brewery worker, and although the committee chose William Wouldhave's design, they decided it should be constructed by a boat-builder, Henry Greathead. He made only one alteration to William's model, by curving the keel slightly, and he gave the boat its name— "The Original". She was 30 feet long and had six pairs of oars. She rose sharply at both bow and stern and had no rudder. But she had a long steering oar at each end, and could be rowed in either direction. She was clinker-built and had cork lining and casings of cork along the

"The Original"—the prototype of the modern life-boat—was designed by William Wouldhave and built by Henry Greathead.

Grace Darling, who became a national heroine after rescuing shipwrecked passengers, has this monument in Bamburgh Churchyard.

Testing the Waveney self-righting life-boat.

Capsized with me strapped inside . . .

. . . totally upside down . . .

and up she comes!

gunwales. "The Original" was first launched on 30 January 1790. A merchant ship got into difficulties as it was making for the Tyne estuary, and that day, the shipwrecked sailors didn't perish—Britain's first life-boat with its crew and local volunteers rescued them all.

By 1801, Henry Greathead had built 21 life-boats like "The Original" and he petitioned the House of Commons for a reward for his invention. He was voted £1200, and even received a diamond ring from Tsar Alexander I of Russia. But although many of William Wouldhave's friends protested, Willy received no reward. He became Clerk of the Parish of St Hilda, and when he died on 28 September 1821, aged 70, his friends erected a gravestone inscribed "William Wouldhave, Clerk of this Church, and inventor of that invaluable blessing to mankind, the life-boat."

Even today, no one is really sure who was more responsible for the success of the life-boat—Wouldhave who designed it, or Greathead who built it. But the Town Council of South Shields thought of a way of honouring them both. They put up a Life-boat Memorial down on the sea front, overlooking the scene of so many rescues. On one side is Greathead's name, and on the other, Wouldhave's. For no one can dispute that between them they laid the foundations of a great service.

More and more people were beginning to recognise the importance of saving life at sea. In 1824, Sir William Hillary formed the Institution for the Preservation of Life from Shipwreck. But it wasn't until 1849 when "The Providence" was wrecked in the Tyne and twenty life-boat men were drowned, that funds poured in. In 1854, the Institution became the Royal National Life-boat Institution.

Although William Wouldhave's design was for a self-righting boat, one great problem that has only recently been solved was how to build a life-boat that was not only self-righting, but also just as stable as the non-self-righting boats. Richard Oakley designed a boat in 1958 that used a clever system of shifting water ballast, but these 37-foot boats could not be fitted with radar without harming the stability so the RNLI designed a new 37-foot class boat that *could* take radar—the Rother life-boat. A new and faster type of life-boat—a 44-foot steel boat—was introduced later, called the Waveney, and with a top speed of 15 knots these self-righting boats are highly manoeuvrable.

But large or small, all life-boats have one aim—to save lives. In May 1974, three members of the crew of our *Blue Peter III* at North Berwick received some of the RNLI's top awards for gallantry after going to the aid of bathers in distress. It's the first time crew members of our Blue Peter boats have received awards and we felt tremendously proud. The RNLI is constantly experimenting and trying to improve its boats and equipment, but rescues couldn't take place without the crews—the gallant volunteers who are well and truly named "The Lifesavers"!

The Award-winning members of *Blue Peter III*.

THE 'WAVENEY' LIFE-BOAT

Length of boat: 44ft 10½ins;
Beam: 12ft 8ins;
Displacement 17 tons;
Maximum speed: 15 knots.

The "Waveney" class life-boats are among the latest types to go into service with the RNLI around the coasts of Britain. Based on a design originally used by the United States Coastguard they are fully equipped for all types of rescue work at sea, and have a range of 180 miles when cruising at 11 knots. Fast and manoeuvrable, the "Waveney" class are self-righting boats, being capable of uprighting themselves in six seconds should they capsize.

1. Steel hull, lined with buoyant foam and shaped to make the boat self-righting.
2. Rubber fenders ranged all around the hull to protect it from bumps.
3. Rope locker containing the mooring rope.
4. Passenger space.
5. Crew's space (shown in the small drawing).
6. Toilet compartment.
7. Stretcher space. This and the passenger space may be used to house survivors.
8. The main mast, with navigation lights, radio aerials flag halyards and a flashing light.
9. The wheelhouse, the position where the boat is "driven".
10. The helm.

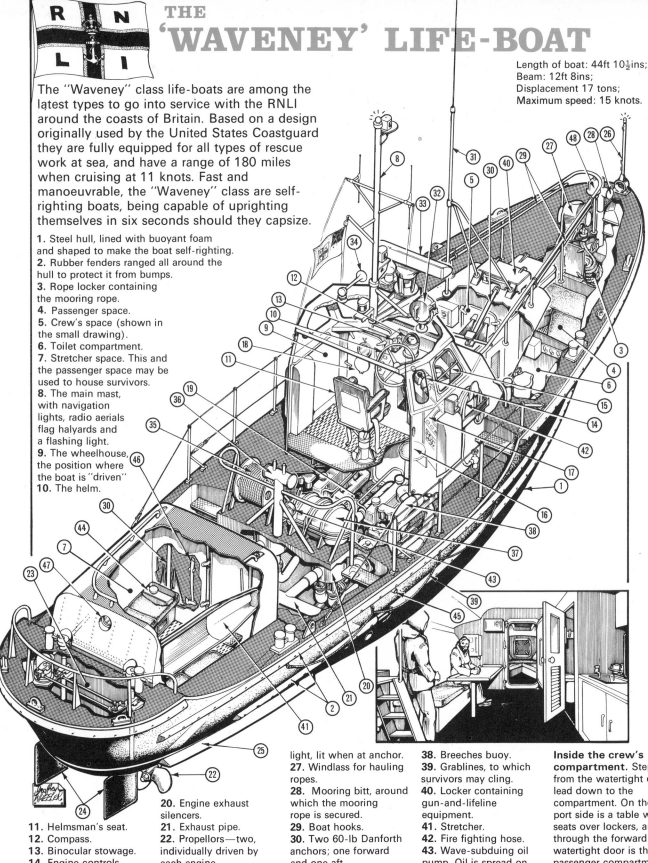

11. Helmsman's seat.
12. Compass.
13. Binocular stowage.
14. Engine controls.
15. Echo sounder display, showing depth of water.
16. Fold-down seat for the navigator.
17. Radar display panel.
18. Watertight door leading to crew's space.
19. Engine compartment containing two 215 horse-power diesel engines.

20. Engine exhaust silencers.
21. Exhaust pipe.
22. Propellors—two, individually driven by each engine.
23. Steering gear compartment.
24. Twin rudders.
25. Trimming tabs, helping to keep the boat steady.
26. Jackstaff and stemhead fairlead (through which the mooring rope may be passed when anchoring etc.). At the top of the jackstaff is the anchor

light, lit when at anchor.
27. Windlass for hauling ropes.
28. Mooring bitt, around which the mooring rope is secured.
29. Boat hooks.
30. Two 60-lb Danforth anchors; one forward and one aft.
31. 18-foot whip aerial for radio equipment.
32. Searchlight.
33. Radar scanner.
34. Horn.
35. Towing rope reel.
36. Towing bitt, around which the towing rope is secured.
37. Six-man inflatable life-raft stowage.

38. Breeches buoy.
39. Grablines, to which survivors may cling.
40. Locker containing gun-and-lifeline equipment.
41. Stretcher.
42. Fire fighting hose.
43. Wave-subduing oil pump. Oil is spread on choppy seas when two boats are trying to draw together and are prevented from doing so by the waves.
44. Subduing oil tank.
45. Subduing oil discharge pipe.
46. Axe.
47. Stern floodlight.
48. Ship's bell.

Inside the crew's compartment. Steps from the watertight door lead down to the compartment. On the port side is a table with seats over lockers, and through the forward watertight door is the passenger compartment with seats and lockers. Lockers contain heaters and are also used for stowing equipment including distress rocke The door on the starbo side opens up the toile compartment with hoo for protective clothing. In the corner is a sink a a water boiler for hot d

TABLE TOP TRIBE

In a forest clearing the braves gather round the flickering camp fire and smoke the pipe of peace. The squaws are busy with the papooses round the brightly decorated wigwams, and a stealthy bear comes to drink at the shimmering lake.

The Forest

1 To make pine trees, start by painting a sheet of plastic foam with dark green poster paint. When it's dry, cut into strips about 40 cm long and wider at the bottom than the top. Fig 1.

2 Cut each strip into a fringe so that it looks rather like a comb. Fig. 2. These strips will form the pine tree branches.

3 The tree trunk is made from a twig, sharpened at one end. Put a dab of rubber solution glue on the point and start wrapping the foam branches round the twig. Push the foam up as you work and when you have wound the branches round about two-thirds of the trunk, stick the end of the foam firmly down with some more glue. Fig. 3. A little bit of brown modelling clay makes a good base.

The Lake

We used a small mirror to make the lake, but if you haven't got one, try a smooth piece of kitchen foil instead. Stick your mirror or foil into the centre of a piece of cardboard. Next put plenty of glue all over the cardboard surround and press some pebbles in to make rocks. While the glue is wet, sprinkle on tiny stones or sand to fill the gaps. Fig. 4. Any bits of green foam that are left over from the trees come in handy here. Snip them into tiny pieces and glue them in among the rocks to make reeds.

And all this can happen on your own kitchen table and pack away in seconds when it's time for dinner.

John and I made this whole scene, forest and all, very easily and very cheaply. If you'd like to make a camp for your Indians too, here's how to do it:

The Wigwams

1 The wigwams are made from brown paper, and as they start out as circles, a tea plate makes a good pattern. Cut out a circle of brown paper and fold it in half. Cut down the fold and you will get two wigwams from each circle. Cut a little half circle in the centre and strengthen the wigwam by glueing on four cocktail sticks. Fig. 5.

2 When the glue is dry and the sticks are firm, put some more glue down one straight edge and fold the wigwam into a cone shape. Decorate the wigwam any way you like. We found gummed paper shapes useful. For the entrance, cut a little way along the glued seam and fold a corner back. The wigwam looks good if you colour the inside of the flap. Fig. 6. By the way, the Indians who lived on the plains called their tents teepees, but the forest tribes of the North called them wigwams, like us.

The Camp Fire

This is the easiest of the lot! Crumple up some red cellophane paper, the kind you get from sweets or in biscuit packets, and stick it to a cardboard base. Build up a camp fire by glueing tiny twigs across it. Position your braves all round it, and the effect is very realistic! Fig. 7.

"Who can ever be tired of Bath?"

wrote Jane Austen in 1801.

There has been a town on the same spot for two thousand years, and the centre of it all is a group of springs of hot water, bubbling out of the earth. There is a strange story told of how the hot springs were first discovered.

In 800 BC the British King Lud Hudibras had a son called Bladud. The prince unfortunately developed leprosy, so he was banished from court and became a swineherd.

Soon the pigs he was looking after got leprosy as well, and Bladud was afraid his master would be angry, so he drove the pigs over the River Avon to find fresh pastures for them.

Suddenly the leading pigs rushed down the hillside, and began to roll and wallow in a muddy bog. Bladud stared at them in amazement, for as they came out of the mud, they were quite better; all the leprosy had gone.

Prince Bladud and the pigs were cured of leprosy by bathing in a spring—and the city of Bath began.

Eagerly Bladud himself plunged into the hot bubbling water in the middle of the bog, and soon he, too, was completely cured.

He hurried back to his father's court and couldn't wait to tell everyone about the healing springs he had discovered.

Prince Bladud was the founder of Bath, for so many people came to visit the healing springs that a town grew up. Bladud's statue still looks down on the Great Bath, where every day half a million gallons of water gush out of the ground at 120 degrees Fahrenheit—as hot as ordinary bath water—in a never-ending stream.

Two hundred years ago people from all over Britain came to Bath to take the waters, to drink them and to bathe in them.

There was a set way for ladies to take a bath; each lady wore a very full gown, with big sleeves. It was yellow, because the mineral salts in the water dyed everything yellow anyway, and it was stiff so that it floated round the lady in the water, without clinging to her. She would step down carefully into the bath, and then she would sit down on a stone, in the water, with just her head sticking out.

Later the Romans took over the town and called it Aqua Sulis.

Bath was at the height of its fashion 200 years ago when elegant streets like Lansdown Crescent were built.

After her bath, the lady would be wrapped in a warm flannel nightgown, and then she would be carried back to her lodgings.

But there was all the rest of the day to get through, before the next morning's bath. People became bored and restless, and didn't know what to do.

It was solved for them by a young man called Richard Nash; he came to Bath and took charge of the social life of the town.

He persuaded the authorities to pave the streets, and lay out gardens for walking. Ballrooms were cleaned and decorated, and Nash drew up a set of rules saying what people should wear and how they should behave.

Now after taking the waters, people found plenty to do to amuse themselves under the eye of Beau Nash, the King of Bath.

Beau Nash changed Bath from a medieval, rough-and-ready town into a centre of fashion. Bath became an institution, and for nearly a hundred years it was the smartest place in England.

The Pump Room, where all the rich, fashionable and important visitors started their day, is still there. Under the crystal chandeliers there is a bubbling fountain of hot water, and those people who didn't want to submit to the rigours of bathing drank three glasses. I tried it—it doesn't taste at all nice, but I suppose everyone felt it must be doing them good, because it was so horrid.

Once that was over, they strolled up and down, and chatted and listened to a band playing. Afterwards they might do some shopping in smart Milsom Street, lined with some of the most elegant shops in the country. The latest fashions for men and women were on display, as they still are, and today many of the shops sell, as antiques, the furniture and glass and china the visitors would have used in their homes.

In the evening, everyone went to the Upper Rooms—the Assembly Rooms, where dances were held, according to Beau Nash's strict rules.

At six o'clock the Ball opened with a minuet.

Bath lies tucked into the folds of the Mendip Hills.

At eight o'clock country dances began, ladies of quality according to their rank standing up first.

About nine o'clock a short interval was allowed for rest and for the gentlemen to help their partners to tea. That over, the company danced

I tried a glass of the famous "Bath waters".

The visitors needed houses to rent for the season so lovely buildings were made out of Bath stone.

The Pump Room, where all the rich and fashionable visitors started their day by taking the waters, is still there today.

until the clock struck eleven.

After dancing ended a little time was allowed for becoming cool, and then the ladies were handed into the sedan chairs.

A Visitors' Book for Bath would include nearly all the famous names in England for more than a hundred years—Queen Charlotte, wife of George III, was an honoured guest; Lord Nelson came here after his victories; John Wesley, the preacher, came to remind the Smart Set they would not live for ever.

And Jane Austen wrote novels about Bath, so that every street and house seems alive with her characters.

All these visitors wanted houses or apartments they could rent for the season, so streets and squares of lovely houses were made out of the golden Bath stone, quarried a few miles away.

Royal Crescent is the loveliest of all, with a great sweep of houses looking down on to the calm beautiful town.

Of course, today, many of these houses are shops or modern flats or offices, but one house in Royal Crescent is the same inside as it would have been when Bath was at the height of its success.

As I explored it I could imagine myself back in those days. In the elegant drawing-room I could almost hear the laughter and talk, the chatting to friends, that was one of the greatest pleasures of Bath.

I walked down the stairs, and in to the library. There is a desk there, and here Jane Austen might have sat, writing those magnificent novels that make the Bath of her times so real for us today.

As one of her heroines says:

"Here there are a variety of things to be seen and done all day long—

"I really believe I shall always be talking of Bath when I am at home again—I do like it so very much.

"Oh, who can ever be tired of Bath?"

THE UGLIEST UGLY SISTERS

Do you remember our Blue Peter Panto? It's certainly something *we'll* never forget in a hurry! We were extremely lucky, because we had panto lessons from none other than Arthur Askey. Arthur's been one of Britain's top comics for half a century—his actual anniversary of 50 years in show business is March 1974—so we couldn't have had a better teacher. Arthur showed us how the jokes and gags in a traditional pantomime are worked out, and how the moves on stage are made. And he gave us tips on our make-up and costumes, too.

We all thought he was extremely kind and patient. Panto always looks so easy on the stage, but it has to be very carefully rehearsed, not only the timing of the lines spoken by the different characters, but the things that Arthur called "the business". That's all the jokey bits where few words are spoken but there's lots of comic action like the Wicked Uncle creeping up behind Aladdin, or Dick Whittington's cat washing his paws, or Baron Hardup's pastry falling on the floor.

It was difficult deciding which panto to choose. There are so many good ones and we all had our favourites. But in the end, we decided on Cinderella. For one thing there are five good parts—Cinders, Prince Charming, the Ugly Sisters and their step-father, the Baron. And it was a hilarious moment when we all dressed up for the first time.

Val's outfit was simple, because Cinders is always in rags until the Ball scene. Lesley looked very glamorous indeed in her Prince Charming gear of long thigh boots, short brocade jacket and superb powdered wig. Arthur was every inch a Baron, although his hat didn't stay on for long. But when Ugly Sisters Cowslip and Buttercup walked in, it was like a bad dream. John and Peter teetered along on six-inch high-heeled shoes. Pete couldn't quite manage his crinoline—it kept falling down and revealing a pair of long, frilly pants with two black handprints in a very prominent position. John's red and white striped woolly stockings didn't seem to match his mauve glitter platform soles— no wonder Petra and Shep were confused—they just couldn't make out what was going on!

Arthur's starred in more pantomimes than we've had hot dinners, so we felt very honoured to have his advice. He told us about all the old traditions, and perhaps it's because a lot of the things people enjoy most in a panto never change, that it's by far the most popular kind of Christmas entertainment.

Pantomime started hundreds of years ago, and in those days the stars of the show were always Harlequin and Columbine, who danced and mimed and never said a word. But today, pantomimes are quite different. They're gorgeous spectacles where tales like Aladdin or Jack and the Beanstalk come to life. Apart from the comedy scenes, full of topical jokes about the latest crises, and often set in rather ordinary places like the kitchen, there are lavish scenes like the ballroom in Cinderella where Cinders arrives

Val and Lesley made a perfect Cinders and Prince Charming. By tradition, in pantomime the part of Principal Boy is always played by a girl, and the Dame is always a man in disguise.

in a coach drawn by real horses, and where the glittering ballroom has a clock about the size of Big Ben! (We missed that scene out in our version!) But perhaps the oddest thing about panto is that although the heroes like Jack,

49

Ugly Sisters Buttercup and Cowslip spend a great deal of the pantomime quarrelling about who's the prettiest.

Peter and John had to learn how to manoeuvre their voluminous crinoline skirts.

Aladdin and Prince Charming are always known as the Principal *Boy*, by tradition they're nearly always acted by *girls*. And in every pantomime there's always a character called the "Dame" like Widow Twankey in Aladdin and Jack's mother in Jack and the Beanstalk, and these parts are played by men. In Cinderella, of course, the men's parts are the Ugly Sisters, and the sight of John and Pete as Miss Cowslip and Miss Buttercup with their low-cut dresses revealing two very hairy chests was unforgettable!

In a way, the rehearsals were even more hilarious than the proper performance, because we didn't have make-up, and only wore half the costumes. For instance, John and Pete wore their high-heeled shoes to get them accustomed to walking in them, and also their crinoline skirts. After wearing trousers all your life, a skirt takes a bit of getting used to, and the hoops holding out the crinoline need a special kind of manoeuvring. So there were the two of them—their faces un-made up—wearing ordinary shirts—but with braces holding up their crinolines—and high-heeled shoes!

Apart from learning how to wear our costumes, Arthur showed us how to say famous lines like the "Oh no you haven't"—"Oh yes I have" joke, which you have to say with a long drawn out "Ohhh no you haven't!"—while the other person replies with an equally long drawn out "Ohhhh yes I *have*!" Then there was the old favourite—the pound note joke—that goes something like this:

UGLY SISTER COWSLIP:	(*to Baron*) You said you'd meet us here.
BARON:	I've been here all the time. *(Ugly sisters wink at each other and give several big nudges)*

UGLY SISTER COWSLIP:	You've been *here*? We're willing to bet you that you're not even here now.
UGLY SISTER BUTTERCUP:	We bet you a pound.
BARON:	Of course I'm here.
UGLY SISTER COWSLIP:	You're not in Scunthorpe, are you?
BARON:	No, I'm not in Scunthorpe.
UGLY SISTER BUTTERCUP	And you're not in Chorlton-cum-Hardy?
BARON:	No.
BOTH UGLY SISTERS:	Well, if you're not in Scunthorpe and you're not in Chorlton-cum-Hardy, then you must be somewhere else?
BARON:	That's right.
BOTH UGLY SISTERS	Well, if you're somewhere else, you're not here! *(Ugly Sisters collapse with laughter while Baron picks up money)*
BOTH UGLY SISTERS:	You've taken our money, that's ours!
BARON:	I haven't taken your money. How can I have taken your money—**I'm not here**! *(General chaos as Ugly Sisters hit each other)*

It's corny jokes like that that make a good pantomime the great fun that it is, and we thoroughly enjoyed learning them from Arthur.

Because we were only doing an excerpt from a pantomime, we had to think of a special ending. And we thought the best thing would be to have a song and dance—so with the lovers, Prince Charming and Cinders, waltzing together, and the

Ugly Sisters looking on jealously we made up this song to the tune of the Last Waltz.

PRINCE CHARMING: (*To Cinders*) I'll have the last waltz with you.
UGLY SISTERS: (*Hugging each other*) Two lonely sisters together.
BARON: (*pointing to Prince Charming & Cinderella*) He fell in love with her.
PRINCE CHARMING, CINDERS, UGLY SISTERS & BARON: } And the last waltz will be for ever.

And because we wanted to have a rousing end for the finale we changed the tune to "Knees Up Mother Brown" and sang this song:

WHOLE CAST: We're getting into practice for going to the Ball.
CINDERS: We'll make sure when we get there—
PRINCE C: Guests will point and guests will stare.
BUTTERCUP: We'll be the prettiest dancers.
COWSLIP: The Prince has ever seen.
BARON: So knees up, knees up, Don't get the breeze up, Keep the party clean!

And we ended with a really strenuous dance with lots of high kicks which John and Pete found quite difficult in their crinolines.

It was all a lot of nonsense, but we really enjoyed ourselves—and that's what Pantomime is all about!

Our Blue Peter Pantomime ended with a rousing song and dance. John and Peter managed *not* to fall over in their high heeled shoes, and Lesley managed *not* to lose her wig!

THE CASE OF THE
GOLDEN CHAMPION

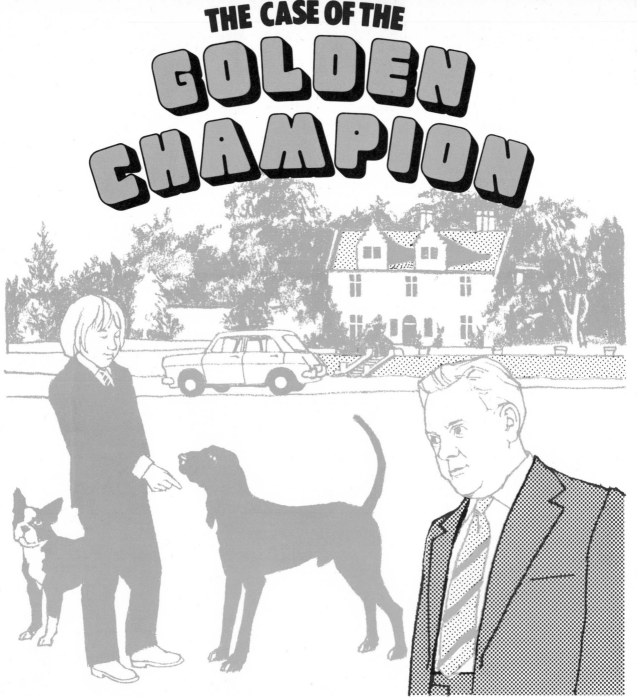

Can you solve this case. Six careless mistakes gave away the crooks. We spotted them. Can you?

"There it is!" cried Bob. "Next on the left. The Woodhouse Kennels".

Detective Inspector McCann turned the car down the gravel drive. As they neared the house, they could see the runs where labrador dogs and puppies of all sizes barked a noisy welcome.

Bob had always been keen on dogs, and he was very much looking forward to visiting this particular kennels—the famous home of champions of his favourite breed. He'd been delighted when his uncle had invited him to come with him on this particular assignment, but all the same, something had worried him ever since he'd left London. Had his uncle, with

his distinguished detection reputation, suddenly been demoted? There was only one way to find out—so he plucked up his courage.

"Er, excuse me mentioning it, Uncle, but has something gone wrong?" he queried tentatively. "It seems strange to me that someone in your position should be wasting your time escorting a dog to France."

"That shows how little you know about dog breeding," laughed his uncle. "This year's Supreme Champion of Wuft's is going to be sold abroad and it's worth a fortune. And as the buyer's a top man in the French government, if anything goes wrong, there'll be an international incident."

As the car ground to a halt, a man in a tweed coat led a superb labrador from an isolated kennel. Carefully he locked the door, slipped the key in his pocket and came towards them.

"Hello," he called. "I see you've got here first."

"Has Monsieur Aubrey Chanteur been delayed?" queried McCann.

"He's just telephoned from the bank—he should be here any second. My name's Mike Bouncer, and this," he said, pointing to the most beautiful golden labrador bitch they'd ever seen, "is Joan of Swithland."

"She's magnificent!" breathed Bob. "No wonder she's the Wuft's Supreme Champion."

While Bob patted the dog, Bouncer drew McCann aside.

"Look here, Inspector," he confided. "I'm not quite sure about this French chappie who's acting as courier for the Minister. That's why I've insisted on being paid in cash, and I'm glad you're here to make sure there's no funny business. We can't have our Joan going off with just anybody!"

At that moment, a Citroen saloon purred up and a black-coated Frenchman stepped out carrying a sleek leather brief-case.

"Doesn't look much of a dog-fancier to me," muttered Bouncer.

"Bonjour, gentlemen," he said. "I am Monsieur Aubrey Chanteur and this, I imagine, is Joan of Swithland. The name reminds me of our famous French Saint Joan of Arc!"

There was no answering smile from Bouncer.

"She's just about the best dog ever to cross the Channel," he snapped. "I hope you know how to look after her on the journey."

"Frankly, Monsieur Bouncer," replied the Frenchman, "I am simply carrying out a commission for my Minister."

"That's the difference between us," countered Bouncer. "I've been breeding dogs for thirty years!"

"Is that so?" said McCann.

"Oh, yes. I had the honour to supply poodles to Her Majesty the Queen. Many's the time I've taken dogs for her approval to Hampton Court Palace."

"How long have you been breeding labradors, then?" queried Bob.

"For about seven years now," replied Bouncer. "Many end up as Guide Dogs for the Blind. They've got an ideal temperament and a sense of colour. This is invaluable when they help their blind owners across the road. They can tell at once when the traffic lights change."

Monsieur Chanteur looked bored. "Shall we get down to business?" he murmured, opening his brief-case. I have the money in one-pound notes, just as you requested."

"No need to hurry," said Bouncer. "I'm more concerned about the dog at the moment. I bet you haven't thought about food for the journey, have you?"

"Er, non, non," said Chanteur, apologetically.

"I thought not! Just as well I've got this bag of well-cooked chicken bones. You'll be able to feed her on the plane."

"You must be pretty experienced in sending dogs by air, Mr Bouncer," said McCann.

"I should say so," the breeder replied. "They know me very well down at Heathrow. Why, I was there only two days ago collecting those three." He pointed to three puppies who were leaping around amongst a pen full of dogs. McCann's interest in his dogs seemed to cheer Bouncer up. He became expansive.

"They came in from Berlin specially for my training. Yes, I'm glad to say I've quite a reputation on the Continent. Now then, Chanteur, let's see the colour of your money!" he laughed.

"I'm very interested in your training methods," persisted McCann, ignoring Bouncer's last remark. "Before we go, would you be so kind as to show my nephew Joan's kennel. I know he'd love to see the kennel of a champion."

Bob looked puzzled, and Bouncer's bonhomie suddenly disappeared.

"I'm afraid you're out of luck. I haven't got time at the moment."

"Oh, surely," said McCann.

"It's no good anyway," Bouncer snapped. "I gave the key to the kennel maid this morning, and she's gone to the village. She may not be back today."

"Try looking in your left-hand jacket pocket," rasped McCann, suddenly moving forward and seizing Bouncer in a vice-like grip.

"Take it, Bob," he cried, "and unlock the kennel door."

"What the devil . . . !" blustered Bouncer.

In a second Bob had the door open. There on the floor, bound and gagged, lay a struggling figure.

"Thank heavens," he breathed, as Bob hurried to release him.

"Mon Dieu!" gasped the Frenchman. "What's going on?"

"You'll find, Monsieur, that that is Joan of Swithland's real owner."

Once again, McCann's detective powers had staggered his nephew.

"But Uncle," he cried. "How did you know the real Mr Bouncer was a prisoner here? I don't understand!"

"And what about him?" queried the equally puzzled Monsieur Chanteur, indicating their erstwhile host, who struggled in the handcuffs McCann had snapped on his wrists.

"I nearly gave him all the Minister's money!"

"He's an impostor," said McCann, gruffly. "He's made six very stupid mistakes—clues that gave away his ludicrous deception. And there's one thing I can promise you, Monsieur," he said as he led the crook away. "It's his turn for the dog house now."

Did you spot the six mistakes? Check your answers on page 76.

The GREAT ESCAPE

1974 is the centenary of the birthday of the world's most famous escapologist—The Great Houdini—whose incredible exploits made him a legend in his own lifetime.

It seemed there was no padlock, chain or iron bar that could hold Houdini, and his escapes baffled audiences all over the world. But although he would never divulge the secrets of his tricks during his lifetime, when Houdini died stories were told that he had given an envelope to his lawyer in New York bearing the message "to be opened on April 6th, 1974". Inside were said to be instructions, telling how all his tricks worked.

Last March, the search began in America, but no envelope could be found. We had hundreds of letters from Blue Peter viewers reminding us of the story, so we, too, joined in the hunt. But with no luck. No one in New York could trace either the envelope or any other papers connected with Houdini. The Great Houdini's tricks remain unexplained!

There are many other strange tales that surround this extraordinary man. For instance, most people think he died performing a spectacular escape from a tank of water with his feet padlocked and bolted into the lid. This *was* Houdini's last trick, but he actually died some time later from an accidental blow to his body.

To mark the anniversary of the birth of this remarkable man, we asked British escapologist Howard Peters if he could reconstruct Houdini's last great escape. Here's what happened in the Blue Peter studio on 18 March 1974.

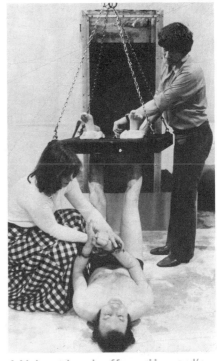

1 Val put handcuffs on Howard's wrists while I padlocked his feet.

2 It was a tense moment as Howard was winched head first into the tank of water.

3 Quickly we unhooked the winch chains and padlocked the lid.

4 Our last glimpse of Howard before the curtains were drawn and his Great Escape began.

5 Forty seconds later Howard was free! But like Houdini, he wouldn't divulge the secret of his trick.

55

RED RECORD SETTERS

On 10 January 1974 Red Setter Settrina Baroness Medina, or Pax for short, became a red *record* setter by producing a litter of 22 pups. She beat the British record previously held by a litter of 21 St Bernards born in 1895, and only missed the world record by one pup. 23 American Foxhounds born in 1945 hold *that*, but even so, Pax's 22 pups were an astonishing achievement.

Pax holds another record, too. As far as we know, she's the only red setter who has given birth attended by three nuns and a Roman Catholic priest. That's because her owner is Monsignor Michael Buckley, the Director of Wood Hall, a Pastoral and Ecumenical Centre near Wetherby in Yorkshire. Monsignor Buckley and the nuns really had their hands full when the pups were born, and it's certainly a day they'll never forget.

Monsignor Buckley said Pax started having her pups at 3.30 on the afternoon of 10 January. It was a Thursday, and by *Blue Peter* time, when we were all in our studio at the Television Centre, Pax had produced six pups. By the 9 o'clock news, she'd had thirteen, and Monsignor Buckley and the nuns sat with her all through the night. By 7 o'clock the next morning, twenty pups had arrived, and Monsignor Buckley said, "Then we went up to Mass, and when

we came down, there was another one!"

Pax had her 22nd and final pup at 2 o'clock on the Friday afternoon, almost 24 hours after pup number one was born!

Unfortunately, one pup was born dead, and six more died after only a few hours, but miraculously, the remaining fifteen survived, and when they visited the studio with Pax, they were all very healthy and lively.

It's not surprising that this record birth caused quite a stir in the local papers. They really hit the headlines in the Yorkshire Post with an article entitled "Nuns and Priest Midwives to Record Litter". And it was very lucky there *was* so much publicity, because it was due to this that Monsignor Buckley was able to find a foster mother to help Pax in her mammoth task of looking after her huge family.

One person who saw that headline was Mr Sydney Gillis of Fryston, and immediately he thought of Nutty, his nine-year-old Collie bitch. After a false pregnancy, Nutty had plenty of milk to spare, so he telephoned Monsignor Buckley and said Nutty might be able to help Pax feed the pups. And she did, together with Sister Gabriel, Sister Imelda and Sister Conrad and all the other nuns at the Centre who fed the pups with milk from fountain-pen fillers.

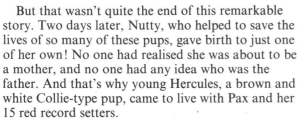

Monsignor Michael Buckley and the nuns who acted as midwives and helped keep the pups alive by feeding them with milk from fountain-pen fillers.

Pax and her pups in the Blue Peter Studio. By this time the puppies were weaned and eating five meals of raw minced beef a day.

But that wasn't quite the end of this remarkable story. Two days later, Nutty, who helped to save the lives of so many of these pups, gave birth to just one of her own! No one had realised she was about to be a mother, and no one had any idea who was the father. And that's why young Hercules, a brown and white Collie-type pup, came to live with Pax and her 15 red record setters.

Nutty, the nine-year-old collie dog, who came to the rescue and acted as foster mother to the pups Pax couldn't feed. After helping to save their lives, Nutty produced just one pup of her own—Hercules—who was completely accepted by his fifteen foster brothers and sisters.

WATT A COLLECTION!

Ever since a cast-off electric light bulb struck Peter Gardiner as too nice to be in the dustbin, he's been fascinated by them. He was four years old when the first one took his fancy. Now, eight years later, he's built up a collection that overflows his home in Desborough, and may well be the first in Britain. So far as we know, his hobby is unique, and we'd never have heard of it if Peter himself hadn't dropped us a line to tell us about it.

He's got over 200 different kinds, ranging from household light bulbs of over 50 different makes, to coloured fairground lights, and a superb set of early motor car lights in a beautiful case. They are 70 years old and still working. Some of the bulbs are still in their original cartons. One of Peter's best is from the 1940s. In those wartime days, there was a shortage of just about everything. Sometimes you had to stand in a queue to get a chance to buy a light bulb, and the carton too wasn't just to be thrown away. Printed on the side there's a reminder that all paper must be kept for salvage.

Peter knows his bulbs so well, he can tell at once the make and type of each one, the differences in the glowing filaments, and the number of units of electricity that they would burn. These are measured in watts, and Peter pointed out that while an ordinary bulb for a bedside light burns about 40, some of the industrial light bulbs in his collection could burn anything up to a thousand.

Although Peter brought only part of his collection to the studio, it made a most impressive display. His Mum and sister came too, lugging great cartons and suitcases of carefully packed glass. But they had even more luggage going home!

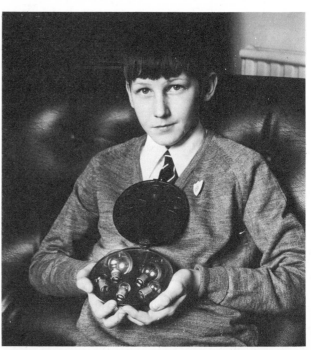

Seventy years old and still working! Peter's superb set of carbon car lamps is still in its original case.

Light bulbs come in all shapes and sizes. Here are just four out of the 200 in the Desborough Illuminations.

1 Spotlight lamp
2 Incandescent lamp
3 1500-watt signalling lamp
4 Tungsten-filament lamp

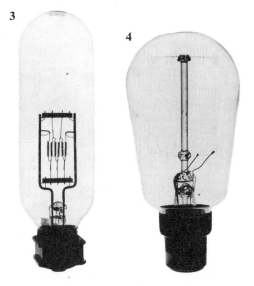

The Blue Peter studio electricians were keen to add to the collection. They produced the biggest bulb Peter had ever seen—the kind that's specially made to light television studios.

It didn't work, but all the same, Peter was delighted. He'd nothing like it in his collection. And as Peter said, perhaps it was just as well that it didn't work. Bulbs like that eat up electricity, and if the Blue Peter lamp had been new, it would have burned 10,000 watts—and the Gardiner family would have had the biggest electricity bill in Desborough!

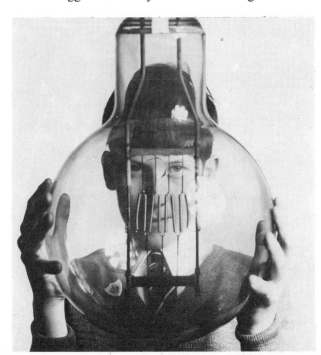

This message pad will last for ever! Provided you write or draw only with a felt-tipped pen, a wipe with a damp sponge will take off every mark. The pad's handy for drawings and messages. Why not make one for a present as well as one for yourself? You can see from these instructions how easy it is.

Write-on Wipe-off!

This is how the drawing-board is put together.

1. The writing surface is made from a detergent bottle. Cut off the top and bottom and cut straight down the tube to make a flat piece of plastic. FIG. 1

2. Soak the plastic in hot water to take the stiffness out. Put glue on the side with writing on and stick the plastic to an oblong of strong cardboard. Don't put it in the middle. Remember to leave a wide border on one side to make room for the sponge and pen holder. For a professional look, round off the corners like I've done. FIG. 2

3. From another piece of strong cardboard, cut a frame for the plastic. It should be the same size as the base, but make the hole smaller than the piece of plastic. This is to hide any rough edges and make a neat job of the frame. FIG. 3

4. To cover the frame, place the cardboard on to a piece of sticky-backed plastic and fold the edges over tidily. To get tidy corners, it helps to snip round the plastic with a pair of scissors. FIG. 4

5. Glue the frame to the base, and if you've got some sticky plastic material left over, cover the back of the board as well. This will make the finished board look nice, as well as strengthen it. Cover a small box with the same material and glue it firmly to the wider piece of the frame. This will hold the felt-tipped pens and a little piece of plastic foam, which makes an excellent sponge. FIG. 5

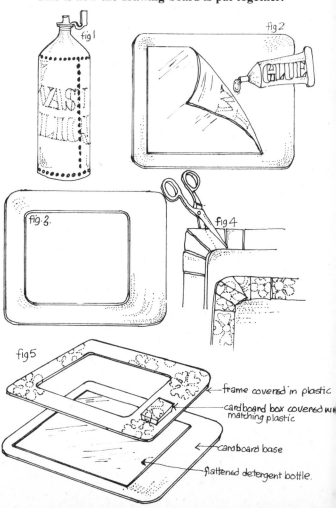

fig 1
fig 2 — GLUE
fig 3
fig 4
fig 5 — frame covered in plastic / cardboard box covered with matching plastic / cardboard base / flattened detergent bottle.

One of our surfing instructors at Newquay was Graham Nile, the European champion.

The other instructor was Tigger Newling, the British champion—so we were in good hands!

"Take care before you start surfing, Peter, because there's just a chance you'll be hooked for life!"

That's what Graham Nile, the European Champion, said to me when Johnny and I joined him on the beach at Newquay in Cornwall. It's without doubt the most "moreish" sport in the world. Perhaps it's because no two waves are ever the same.

"When you come off, you always think the next wave is going to give you the run of a lifetime," said Graham.

"And if you get the run of a lifetime . . . ?" I asked.

" . . . then you can't wait to do it again!" he said.

Coming in to meet us on a great, towering wave was Tigger Newling, the British Champion. He stood poised on the board with his knees bent; then suddenly he changed direction and streaked diagonally across the side of the great, green wave. For a second he bent so far backward that he seemed certain to fall, but by a miracle of balance he righted himself and came roaring in on the white water as the wave splashed on to the beach.

"He's one of the best in Europe on the backhand," said the champion admiringly.

Johnny looked a bit doubtful.

"Somehow I don't think I'll be able to do that," he said.

"Don't worry, we'll start you on the soup where it's easy," said Graham.

The "soup" is the white water, after the wave has broken. The "green" is the green sheer side of the wave as it comes roaring from the Atlantic.

We had the beach all to ourselves which wasn't surprising on a freezing cold November day. Wet suits have made surfing an all-the-year-round sport, even in Northern Europe.

Surfing began at Malibu in California, although people say that the South Sea Islanders have been doing it since time began. The surf board used today is usually made of fibre-glass. It's about two metres long with rounded ends and a plastic fin which sticks out at the back. The fin works like the keel on a boat, without it you'd slide about all over the wave. There's an ankle strap attached to a piece of rope on each board.

"That's for when you fall off," said Graham. "It stops the board from getting away and clouting the guy in front."

Before you start surfing, you have to get out to where the waves are breaking, and that means lying face down on the board and paddling with both hands through the oncoming waves. You

John was the first to stand up—just for ten seconds.

The photographer had to be quick to catch me as well.

need to be really fit to burrow through the great Atlantic rollers and still have enough energy to turn round and surf back.

We had beginners' boards which are about three metres long, and supposedly easier to stand up on. The idea is to wait until you see a good wave coming, and then paddle like fury staying just in front of where the wave is breaking. It's a great moment when you feel caught in that unstoppable thrust from behind, with your right knee up on the board—then your left foot—then—crash! You're being bowled over and over—under the water—with the board tugging impatiently on your ankle.

We emerged out of the boiling foam and forced our way back through the waves to have another go. After about twenty disasters I actually managed to stand up for about a second before I fell over—again!

"Good, Pete!" shouted Graham above the roar of the sea. "But you're standing too far back on the board —get farther forward."

"Choose the big ones, Johnny," Tigger shouted. "It's easier to stay up with power behind you."

After about half an hour, I knew I didn't have the strength to go out again. Johnny and I staggered up the beach, leant on our boards and looked enviously at Graham and Tigger riding the green water.

"D'you think it's as good as free falling, Johnny?" I asked him.

The lad from Halifax grinned.

"I don't know," he said. "We haven't really tried it yet, have we?"

RAT-TAIL & CHIPS

How would you like Rat·tail fish fingers-Thorn Back Ray and chips -or Rabbit Fish?

They may all be on our menus soon as Britain's trawlers search for fish in deeper and deeper waters. The shortage of familiar fish like cod, haddock and plaice means the trawlermen are looking for substitutes, and so far, more than twenty unusual varieties have been found as far as 500 fathoms or 3000 feet deep—that's more than twice the normal trawling depth.

Experts who have eaten these strange creatures say rat-tail—or grenadier as it's also called—and black scabbard are the most tasty. But as most of the deep-water fish are pretty hideous-looking with bulging eyes, gaping jaws and rough, spiky bodies, they'll probably be processed and turn up in the shop as fish cakes or fingers. Here's what they look like *before* they're turned into our dinners!

Blue Ling

Rat-tail

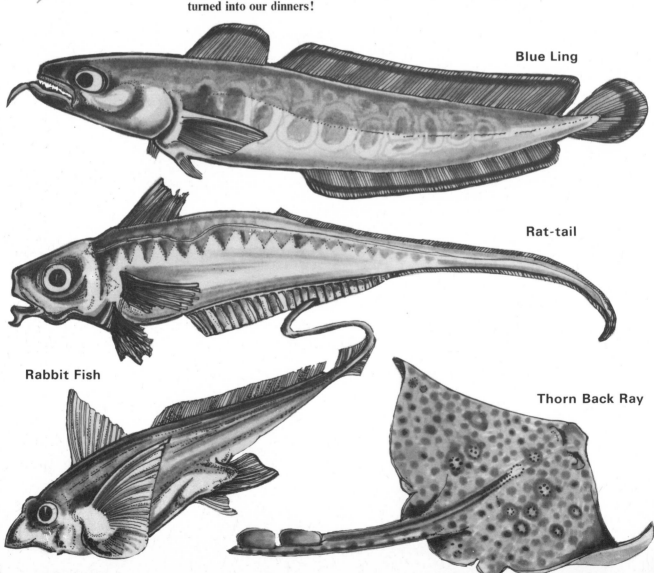

Rabbit Fish

Thorn Back Ray

Here's an idea for turning old Christmas or birthday cards into a game for any number of players.

The idea is to "fish" for the fish in the tank. Each fish has a number, and the fisherman with the top score is the winner.

You're Hooked!

① fold old card in two and glue together

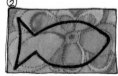

② draw outline of a fish on each card

③ cut out 20 or 30 fish draw in features; eyes, mouth & tail.

④ make a hole in the centre of each head. Thread some fusewire through and twist into a loop

put a number on each fish

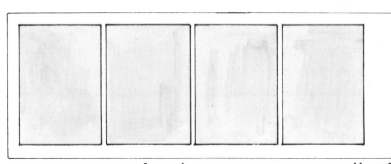

Rods:
Cut off the fronts of the taller cards, roll them firmly over and over into a rod shape and glue down the final fold. Cut a slit in one end and slip in a piece of string about 20cm (8") long.
Tie a knot at one end to hold the string in place and tie a piece of fuse wire bent into a hook on to the other end.

Aquarium:
Glue four cereal packet sides on the sheet of wrapping paper, leaving a small gap between each and a larger one at one end.
Turn the edges of paper (except the wide edge) in and glue down. Stand the cards up on end and fold to make a "box" shape. Glue the wide edge of paper down to complete the box. If there are any cards left over, cut out more fish shapes and glue on the sides for decoration.

How To Play:
Put all the fish into the aquarium and try to fish them out with the rods without looking! Points are scored according to the numbers on the fish. The person who "catches" the highest number of points is the winner. You can make the game even more difficult by making the hooks smaller on the fish with the high numbers.

Way back in 1837, a young man called
George Tutill decided to give up his life as a
travelling showman and settle down.
He opened a business and very soon
advertisements like this began to appear.

GEORGE TUTILL,
83, CITY ROAD, LONDON.

INVENTOR AND SOLE PATENTEE
of the
MAGNIFICENT WOVEN BANNERS
With Scroll and Ornamental designs woven in the silk, and APPROPRIATE PAINTINGS ON
BOTH SIDES to order.
AND MANUFACTURER OF THE
PATENT INDIARUBBER SILK (in One Piece, Without Seams),
PAINTED ON BOTH SIDES WITH ARTISTIC DESIGNS, SUITABLE FOR ANY SOCIETY.
ALSO THE ACTUAL MANUFACTURER OF
Artistic and Durable Regalia of every description
FOR ALL SOCIETIES.

BANNER ★ MAKER

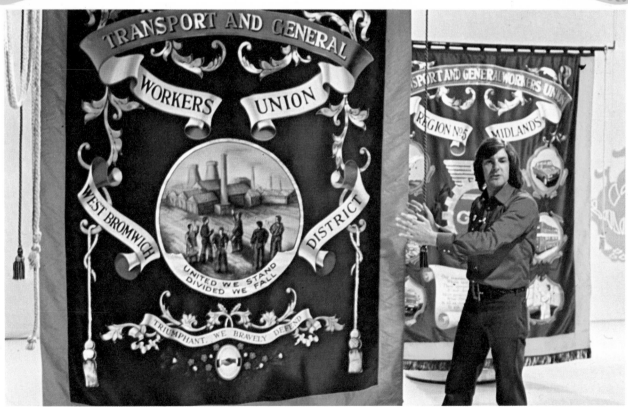

The biggest buyers of George's Patent India Rubber
Silk turned out to be the newly-formed Trade Unions.
Each group of men wanted a banner to carry through
the streets which would show instantly who they were
and what trade they followed. George designed and
made them banners as bright and colourful as the
fair-ground signs he'd painted as a boy. The silk
banners were enormous, as we discovered when we
borrowed some to show in the studio. They were
heavy, too, and although we could lift them all right
indoors, it's said that if the weather was bad and

windy, it took at least six men to carry them.

Today the tradition of Unions having banners is
still going strong, and on big occasions like the
Durham Miners' Gala, literally dozens of them are
carried in procession. But 140 years ago, that
couldn't have happened. In those days Unions were
secret societies, and to join one meant taking a
desperate risk. But some men felt their lives so
hopeless that the risk was worth taking. They became
known as the Tolpuddle Martyrs—and this is their
story.

TOLPUDDLE MARTYRS

1 "Hedging and ditching
To plough and to reap.
How can a man live
On eight shillings a week?"
That was the rhyme the farm labourers chanted as they toiled long hours for low wages.

2 Eight shillings a week! George Loveless of Tolpuddle in Dorset found it impossible. He struggled hard to feed his family, but they were near starvation—potatoes were all they could afford to eat.

3 Bravely, George went to the farmers to ask for more money for the labourers. He was a clever man who had taught himself to read and write and he put the case so well that the farmers promised to put up the wages to ten shillings. It seemed a miracle!

4 But the promise was never kept. The weeks went by and the wages stayed down. And then the farmers said, "Eight shillings is too much. We can only afford to pay six."

5 The men were desperate and looked to George for leadership. 'We cannot live honestly on such scanty means," said George. "I shall write to a big Society in London and perhaps they will help us."

6 Not long after some men came to Tolpuddle on the coach from London. They were officers of the Society which was called The Grand National Consolidated Trade Union. "We'll back you up," they said, "but our Union has enemies. You must swear to keep our secrets and our rules."

7 So that night, the Tolpuddle men met secretly at George's cottage. There was George and his brother, their sister's husband, Thomas Standfield, and his son John, young James Brine, James Hammett—and William Legg. And they all swore a solemn oath of loyalty to the Union.

8 But the Squire and the vicar and the farmers heard about it. It was William Legg who told them! They were furious and wrote to complain to the Government that their labourers were banding together.

9 The Government said it was not a crime to ask for more wages—even for a Union. But they also said it was a crime to take an oath of loyalty to anyone except the King.

10 On a cold February morning, George Loveless was arrested as he set off for work. He was told he had broken the law—he had taken an oath *against* the King. George's friends were taken to prison, too.

The trial went badly. The jurymen were [far]mers and landowners, men who themselves [pai]d scant wages to their labourers. And [wo]rst of all, William Legg gave untruthful [evi]dence against them. "Guilty!" said the [Jud]ge.

12 George and his friends were sentenced to transportation. That meant that for seven years they were to work as convicts on the other side of the world. They knew that many men died in the convict settlements and they might never see their homes or families again.

Then one day, in far off Van Diemens land, George Loveless came [up]on an old newspaper. It said that the cruel treatment of the [Tol]puddle men had shocked so many people that the King [him]self had pardoned them!

14 A coach bowled along the road from Dorchester to Tolpuddle. It was the return journey for the men who, four years before, had trudged that same road under arrest and going to their trial. Now they were going home!

In Tolpuddle, their wives and families and all the village waited for them. [No]w they were celebrities, known throughout the country as the [To]lpuddle Martyrs, who had suffered to make it possible for ordinary men [to] join together to improve their working lives and the lives of their [fa]milies.

SCONE PIZZA

QUESTION What has Princess Anne's wedding got to do with my Scone Pizza?

ANSWER I said give your Mum a rest and let her put her feet up and watch the wedding on the telly while you made my Scone Pizza for her dinner — which is what hundreds of Blue Peter viewers did! And I'm glad to say my Scone Pizza was a great success. Judging by the letters you wrote, even Fanny Cradock would have been proud of the testimonials I received!

Joking apart, it's a really simple recipe that's great for using up left-overs. I like mine hot, but the pizzas are quite tasty cold, too, which makes them useful for picnics as well as TV snacks.

These are the ingredients you will need:

For the scone mixture:
8 oz self-raising flour
2 oz fat—any hard fat will do, but don't use a soft margarine
a pinch of salt and some pepper
a little milk
a little extra fat for cooking
For the toppings I used:
onion rings—partly cooked
scraps of cooked bacon
cheese, chopped tomato, hard-boiled egg and sardines.

After sieving the flour into a bowl, add the salt and pepper; next add the fat, rubbing it into the flour using your fingers, until the mixture looks like breadcrumbs. This takes about 30 seconds.

Begin stirring the milk in—*don't* add too much at first—and mix until you have a sticky dough which will hold its shape. Melt some fat in the bottom of a frying pan and put the mixture in, levelling it out with a wooden spoon. Cook on a medium heat until the underside is done— about ten minutes.

Using a slice, turn the scone over and cook for about another ten minutes. (If you want to cook the scone in the oven, put the mixture into a greased baking tin and cook in a pre-heated oven— Gas Mark 8 or 450°F.—for 12 to 15 minutes or until it has risen and is a golden brown.) By the way, if you're not allowed to use a stove yet, you will need some help from an adult with the cooking. If you are using the stove remember to keep the pan handle turned away so that there is no danger of knocking it over or of any young members of the family being able to reach it.

While the scone is cooking, prepare the topping. Slice the onion into rings and pre-cook them in a little fat until they're clear but not brown. Slice the cheese, chop the cooked bacon into small pieces and cut up the tomatoes (they can be tinned ones)—or hard boil your eggs and open your tinned sardines. Arrange the topping on your Scone Pizza, making sure you leave the cheese until last.

Finish your Scone Pizza off by cooking it under a medium grill for about ten minutes *or* put it back in the hot oven, on the top shelf, for ten minutes.

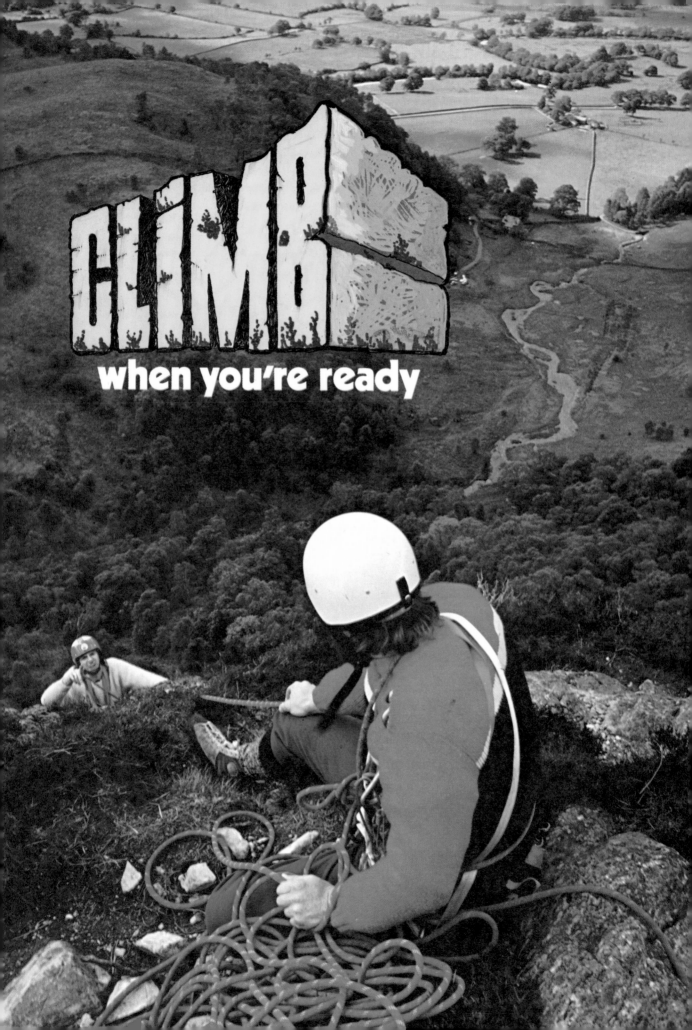

2 My climbing partner was Chris Bonnington, one of the world's top mountaineers.

3 We had to walk half a mile before we came to the bottom of the crag.

4 Gear is very important. This is the truss that my rope is attached to.

"Climbing"

"Aye Aye"

These words are spoken by mountaineers every time they begin to climb, and the words are vital. A misunderstanding on the rock face can cost a life.

I think the ascent of Black Crag with Chris Bonnington is just about the best thing that's happened to me since I joined Blue Peter. I was born in North Lancashire and I've loved the Lake District all my life. I've done quite a bit of modest rock climbing in my time, but I never thought I'd be good enough to attempt Black Crag. I'd often seen it from across the shimmering lake of Derwentwater—a massive grey wall of rock rearing up out of the green trees. But even my very

5 And our lives depended on that rope, so Chris spent a long time sorting it out.

6 Modern climbing boots called "P.A.s" are lightweight and made of canvas and rubber.

7 Halfway up the first pitch and already it's hard climbing.

8 For some footholds, I had to lift my leg level with my waist.

9 "Move your left leg a foot to your right," called Chris.

wildest dreams didn't take me on an expedition to the summit with Chris Bonnington, one of the greatest mountaineers in the world, for a climbing companion.

Chris believes that a good mountaineer never takes risks! That may sound silly when the whole sport is one great big risk, but according to Chris, mountaineering is safe, providing you've got the knowledge and the right equipment.

Ropes are the most important—your life quite literally hangs on them. Your rope is tied to a special webbing truss that is secured through your legs as well as round your waist. The boots were surprising; not great, thick, heavy studded leather boots, but lightweight rubber-soled "P.A.s" that make you feel the contours of the rock.

"You almost stick to the sheer rock face with those on," said Chris.

The crash helmet is vital. A piece of rock the size of a pea is like a bullet when it falls from 300 feet.

An assault on a rock face must be planned like a military operation. There are about twenty different routes up the crag, and the one Chris had chosen was graded in the climbing books as "very severe/mild", which meant it was easy for Chris, but I was going to be fully stretched.

The best climber always goes first, but that wasn't a difficult decision! Chris moved confidently up to the end of the first pitch.

"Taking in," he called down to me, and began to pull up the slack on the rope between us.

"That's me," I called back as I felt the rope tighten.

Chris took a belay round a convenient rock and shouted.

"Climb when you're ready!"

"Climbing," I said, sticking my toe into a tiny foothole.

"Aye, Aye," called Chris.

A belay means a tying of the rope round a rock so that the rock will take the strain if the climber falls off. At that moment, it didn't seem all that unlikely!

I was only six feet off the ground, but already I was fighting for every move.

"Think every time before you do it," called Chris from above. "It's quite straightforward if you look what you're doing."

Somehow I made the ledge where Chris was sitting. I felt as though I'd climbed the north face of the Eiger.

"That was quite an easy one, Pete," he said looking upwards. "It's the last pitch that's the really tricky one."

Pitch 2 is 80 feet of almost sheer rock face. Chris went first again, this time it was up to me to make the belay round the rock, so that if Chris fell I would be able to hold him. I watched every foothold and handhold Chris used, hoping I'd be able to remember them all.

"It's easier than it looks, Pete," he called reassuringly. "Make your feet do the work, and always keep three of your limbs in contact with the rock."

10 The foot of the third pitch—now I was beginning to feel the height.

Soon it was my turn again.

Half-way up the second pitch, my arms were aching and my knees began to feel wobbly. For a second I couldn't think what to do. My heart began to pound in my ears.

"Don't panic, Purves," I whispered out loud. "Panic uses up energy, and you haven't got any to spare."

"Nicely, Pete," called Chris calmly. "Lift your left foot up another six inches and you'll find a lovely hold."

My toe rubbed along the vertical step—nothing A bit higher—still nothing. Bump, bump, bump went my heart.

"Come on, higher still," called Chris.

My toe slipped into the crevice.

"There you are—well done!"

I was moving again!

Pitch 3 was easier, but not a moment to relax.

"It's when you start taking a mountain for granted that you find she'll hit back again," Chris warned. All Lake District crags can be treacherous. There may be plenty of handholds, but there are plenty of loose rocks as well, and a slip on the easy section is just as dangerous as a slip on the sheer cliff.

But the last pitch was something else. The first part was not too bad, but just before the summit there was a massive overhang. I stood looking up and watched Chris disappear from view as he rounded the pinnacle. I've never felt more alone in all my life. But a few seconds later the voice came floating down the mountain.

"Climb when you're ready!" I cleared my throat.

"Climbing," I called.

"Aye Aye," said the voice.

Slowly, and by now quite painfully, I rounded the overhang, and there was Chris, beaming all over his face.

"You've done it," he said. "You've reached the summit of your Everest!"

It was every bit as hard—for me, anyway— that overhang!

"That's what I like about climbing," said Chris. "As long as you're fully stretched, then you're enjoying yourself."

I turned and looked at Derwentwater laid out before us with the mountains and the endless blue sky stretching away to eternity.

"What a view!" I said.

"It's as lovely as anywhere in the world," said Chris.

And that's what climbing's all about!

11 Chris, the leader, appeared on the crest of Black Crag.

12 "Climb when you're ready," called Chris for the last time.

13 "You've done it," said Chris. "You've reached the summit of your Everest!"

14 When you reach the top, you know what climbing's all about.

SOLUTIONS

PUZZLE PICTURES

1. This **ship** was presented to Blue Peter by **Kenneth Rowden of County Durham**, who came to the studio to show how his intricate metal sculpture was made.
2. The **Roman Pavement** at **Woodchester** is Europe's largest Roman mosaic. It lies 1½ metres under the soil in the graveyard of Woodchester Church and is uncovered once every ten years.
3. Lesley rode **Melody Fair** when **Harvey Smith** gave her some jumping lessons.
4. Ten minutes after this photograph was taken, John drove this strange vehicle through the studio wall! It was **a scooter invented to save petrol and could clock up an amazing 450 miles to the gallon.**
5. Another weird vehicle—**Dr Who's car.**
6. During Val's Special Assignment in Madrid, she discovered **how to drink wine from a Porron**—an all-in-one bottled glass. Christopher Dominguez from Seville gave us all a Spanish drinking lesson—with mixed results!
7. John was padded up to the eyebrows when he joined the **London Lions Ice Hockey team.**
8. **Dyking boots** like these were worn by peat diggers and ditch cleaners as recently as the beginning of this century. This pair came from a farm near Weymouth and are on display at the Street Shoe Museum.
9. **A giant guy** built for the Picketts Lock Centre fireworks display by designers Gareth Ball and Peter Kuttner.
10. **Sarah, a three-month-old baboon,** who had been hand reared after being abandoned by her mother at a Safari Park.
11. The boys of **The Tucsan Arizona choir** not only sang, they performed spectacular rope tricks, too.
12. **Paco Pena's Flamenco Pura** set all our feet tapping when they played and danced in the Blue Peter Studio.

THE CASE OF THE GOLDEN CHAMPION

1 Bouncer said he supplied poodles to the Queen, but Her Majesty is famous for her corgis.
2 Hampton Court Palace is no longer a royal residence, so Bouncer would not have taken dogs there to show to the Queen.
3 Bouncer said the Guide Dogs were able to distinguish the colours of the traffic lights. This is not true—dogs cannot understand traffic lights.
4 As any dog lover knows, you should never give cooked chicken bones to an animal because they may choke on the splinters.
5 Big dogs, like labradors, are not allowed to travel with their owners on planes. They must stay in the freight compartment, so Bouncer should have known that Mr Chanteur could not feed Joan titbits on the journey.
6 By law, all dogs must go into quarantine for six months when they are admitted to the United Kingdom. Bouncer must have been lying when he said he'd brought three puppies from Berlin a few days previously.

BIDDY BAXTER EDWARD BARNES AND ROSEMARY GILL WOULD LIKE TO ACKNOWLEDGE THE HELP OF GILLIAN FARNSWORTH, MARGARET PARNELL, EILEEN STRANGE AND JOHN STRANGE

USEFUL INFORMATION

Blue Peter Books

Blue Peter Royal Safari
Blue Peter Book of Limericks
Blue Peter Special Assignment
London, Amsterdam & Edinburgh
Blue Peter Special Assignment
Rome, Paris & Vienna
Blue Peter Special Assignment
Venice & Brussels
Blue Peter Special Assignment
Madrid, Dublin & York
Paddington's Blue Peter Story Book

Blue Peter Inshore Life Boats

Blue Peter I —Littlehampton (a 21-foot Atlantic boat) Secretary: Peter Cheney, Tel: Littlehampton 3922

Blue Peter II —Beaumaris (a 16-foot Inshore Rescue boat shortly to be replaced by a 21-foot Atlantic boat) Secretary: M. L. Booth, Tel: Beaumaris 589

Blue Peter III —North Berwick (A 16-foot Inshore Life boat) Secretary: J. D. Tweedie, Tel: North Berwick 2963

Blue Peter IV —St Agnes (a 16-foot Inshore Life boat) Secretary: C. J. Whitworth, Tel: St Agnes 850

PLEASE TELEPHONE TO CHECK ON INDIVIDUAL BOATHOUSE OPENING HOURS

Royal National Life Boat Institution
42 Grosvenor Gardens, London S.W.1.

Ivory Coast Embassy,
1 Upper Belgrave Street, London S.W.1.

Dewi II
3rd (Volunteer) Battalion, The Royal Regiment of Wales, Cardiff.

RAF Falcons,
RAF Abingdon, Berks.

Bath Information Bureau,
Pump Room, Bath, BA1 1LZ

British Surfing Association,
Bournemouth Road, Parkstone, Poole, Dorset.

British Mountaineering Council,
70, Brompton Road, London S.W.3

Street Shoe Museum,
Street, Somerset.   Curator: Miss Elaine Dyer.
Tel: Street 3131
Open 10.00—1.00 p.m.
2.00—4.45 p.m.

ACKNOWLEDGEMENTS

"Who can ever be tired of Bath?" was written by Dorothy Smith; *Tolpuddle Martyrs* and the illustration on page 45 were by Robert Broomfield; *Bleep & Booster* and the *Mystery Picture* by "Tim"; *The Case of the Golden Champion* was illustrated by Bernard Blatch; *The Waveney Life Boat* by Geoffrey Wheeler.

Photographs in this book were taken by:
Joan Williams, Charles Walls, Barry Boxall, John Jefford, Barnaby's Picture Library, J. Allan Cash, Camera Press, Royal National Life Boat Institution, John Adcock, Bill Campbell, Mike Coles, Rosemary Gill, Malcolm Hill, John E. Jenbrow, Peter R. Smith, Ken Westbury, and the Yorkshire Post.

The George Tutill advertisement on page 66 is from the John Gorman collection.

The cover photograph and those taken during "The Long Fall" are reproduced by kind permission of the Ministry of Defence (Crown Copyright).

BLUE PETER COMPETITION

Would you like to meet Valerie, John, Peter, Lesley and the rest of the Blue Peter team? Would you like to see all the animals? Would you like to come to London and have tea with them all? This is your chance!

The first prize will be an invitation to an exciting

BLUE PETER PARTY

and there will be lots of competition badges for the runners-up, too.

We've been lucky enough to travel all over the world on our Blue Peter Expeditions and we've visited lots of foreign countries.

Here are pictures taken in eight of them. Can you recognise the countries? Their names are included in this list:

MEXICO MOROCCO ICELAND DENMARK JAMAICA ETHIOPIA
CEYLON GERMANY FIJI AMERICA AUSTRIA
IVORY COAST TONGA NORWAY

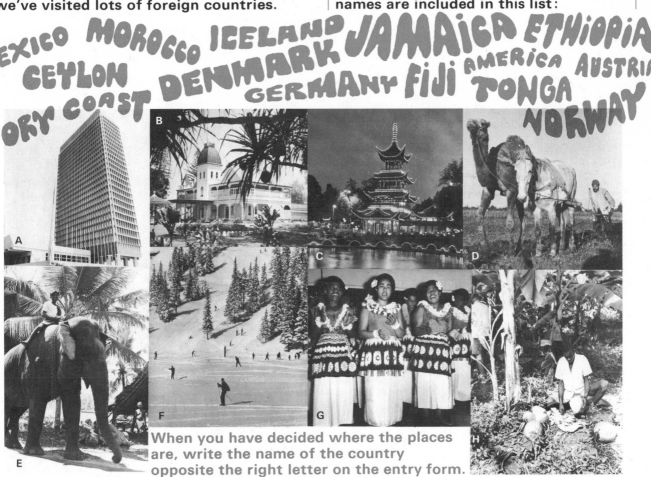

When you have decided where the places are, write the name of the country opposite the right letter on the entry form. To start you off, we've filled one in for you.

A ....
B ....
C ....
D ....
E ....
F ....
G ....Fiji..........
H ....

Cut out your entry and send it to:
Blue Peter Competition, BBC TV Centre, London W12 7RJ.

Name _____ Age _____

Address _____

_____

First-prize winners and runners-up will be notified by letter.
The closing date for entries is 10 January 1975.